GHOSTS AND
LEGENDS
OF THE
VEGAS VALLEY

GHOSTS AND LEGENDS
OF THE
VEGAS VALLEY

HEATHER LEIGH, PHD

FOREWORD BY REVEREND SHAWN PATRICK WHITTINGTON

Haunted America

Published by Haunted America
A Division of The History Press
Charleston, SC
www.historypress.com

Front cover: Bellagio Hotel & Casino as seen from a room in the Paris Las Vegas Hotel & Casino. *Heather Leigh*.
Back cover: *Heather Leigh*; *inset*: *Heather Leigh*.

First published 2023

Manufactured in the United States

ISBN 9781467153317

Library of Congress Control Number: 2022947157

Notice: The information in this book is true and complete to the best of our knowledge. It is offered without guarantee on the part of the author or The History Press. The author and The History Press disclaim all liability in connection with the use of this book.

To my crazy family, who always supports my crazy ideas and sometimes follows me on our ghostly adventures. Love you, Josh, Aidan, Papa, Mama and Liam!

I also wrote this book in memory of Peter James "Pete" Haviland (2/11/67–11/22/21), who was a fantastic mentor and inspiration in paranormal research. He pushed me to finish and submit my first book, Haunted Southern Nevada Ghost Towns. *I will always be grateful that he considered me a friend. Miss you, Pete! Until we meet again.*

CONTENTS

FOREWORD

So, two ghosts are sitting in a jail cell. The first ghost says to the other ghost, "Disturbing the peace. You?" The second ghost responds, "Possession!"

That's as supernaturally silly as I'm going to get here. Maybe.

Ghost bustin' is serious biz! So, if you are in Las Vegas Valley getting your ghost hunt on and you capture an odd EVP that says, "Too legit to quit," the ghost is probably talking about the author of this book.

My conversation with Heather went something like this:

> *Heather Leigh: "Hey Shawn, it's Heather."*
> *Shawn: "Heather, who?"…Lol. (Just kidding.) "You mean the Ghost Lady, Miss Haunted USA, Head Schoolmaster at Ghost ED 101, Exploration Paranormal, THAT Heather?"*

The point I am trying to make here is that the only person qualified to write this book is my friend Heather Leigh Carroll-Landon. She knows that I love and respect her. It is a shame that there are not many more like her in the paranormal community.

This book brings back memories for me of the many paranormal amber alerts I conducted at Fox Ridge Park, the Bible gifted to me by a ghost at the Apache Hotel and the time I spent the whole night at La Palazza with other ghost hunters, only to find myself the only man left standing when the sun came up. And on and on.

Trust me, if there is an unofficial list floating around of the most haunted cities in America and Las Vegas is not at the top of that list, we need to redo that list, put Las Vegas at the top and make the list official! Heather is well on her way to doing just that with this book.

If you are a ghostbuster, ghost hunter, paranormal investigator or just passionate about the paranormal, this book needs to be in your personal library. If you are a nonbeliever, a diehard skeptic or even an annoying parapsychologist, you should get the book, too! We won't tell on you—remember, what happens in Vegas stays in Vegas. Unless you're not careful and end up with a spirit attachment that will follow you home and might leave a mark. Most importantly, respect the locations, respect the ghosts and learn to laugh a little, especially at yourself!

Enjoy the book!! Well done, Heather!

God bless.

—Shawn Patrick Whittington (Seminarian)
United States Old Catholic Church

ACKNOWLEDGEMENTS

Several people contributed to the success of *Ghosts and Legends of the Vegas Valley*, including my husband, Josh, and my son, Aidan, who both went exploring with me to discover new haunted locations.

A huge shoutout goes to Reverend Shawn Patrick Whittington, who wrote an amazing foreword. I am lucky to have a friend like him.

Brian Rollins has helped again with one of my books, this time contributing an amazing story about Green Valley Park in Henderson, Nevada, and fantastic photos to go with it.

Ryan MacMicheal also contributed again, with some amazing photos and stories from his website honoring the memories of the beloved pets buried at the Boulder City Pet Cemetery.

Finally, I want to thank Philip Luna and Cindy Liberatore for allowing me to investigate and learn more about the history of mining in southern Nevada. McCaw School of Mines in Henderson is truly an amazing place.

Showgirls in front of the historic Las Vegas sign. *Library of Congress*.

Introduction

When it comes to ghosts, demons, aliens and other supernatural beings, what happens in Vegas is best left in Vegas. In comparison, the glitz, glamour and gambling pales to all of the paranormal activity reported in Sin City and throughout the Vegas Valley region. Nevertheless, the high excitement and energy have fueled ghosts, spirits and out-of-this-world entities to manifest and make themselves at home.

Since its inception, the Vegas Valley has played host to high-ranking members of the mob, washed-up entertainers, eccentrics and disillusioned dreamers who believed with all their hearts that Las Vegas was the perfect place for their new start. Several spirits lurking in the shadows belong to the many people who helped shape Sin City into its magnificent destination. Joining these spirits include those people who died in the area, shed blood and tears to make a living in Las Vegas or are just popping in to see what the lights and excitement are all about.

It is not uncommon to walk down the Las Vegas Strip and pass by a ghost or even an otherworldly creature and not even know it. There is so much happening in the central area of Las Vegas that it is easy to suffer from sensory overload and miss out on the subtle hints of supernatural activity. Even when you know what to look for, it is easy to miss some ghostly occurrences. In most cases, the spirits in the Vegas Valley like to be left alone. However, some spirits cause such a ruckus that guests are forced to check out in the middle of the night.

Above: Daytime aerial view of the Strip. *Library of Congress*.

Left: Nighttime aerial view of the Strip. *Library of Congress*.

Historic Vegas neon sign, Fremont Street. *Library of Congress.*

So it is best not to try too hard to look for paranormal activity, because if they want you to know they are there, trust me, they will find a way to let you know. As any paranormal researcher can tell you, paranormal activity typically occurs when you least expect it, especially when the cameras are turned off.

Las Vegas is one of the most haunted locations in America's western region, and the desolate surrounding landscape provides an eerie backdrop to some of the creepiest paranormal accounts in the world.

I hope you enjoy this book, which takes you into the supernatural world with stories of ghosts, spirits, inhuman entities and UFOs shared throughout the Vegas Valley.

PART I
LAS VEGAS

1

BALLY'S LAS VEGAS HOTEL
AND CASINO

A tragic incident occurred on the Las Vegas Strip on November 21, 1980, around 7:00 a.m. Emergency services received a call about a fire at the MGM Grand Hotel and Casino, which is now the location of Bally's Las Vegas Hotel and Casino.[1] Fire investigation reports state that the blaze started in the deli and quickly spread throughout the casino floor. The fire injured hundreds of people, and the smoke and toxic fumes filling the air killed eighty-five. An additional two victims died later at the hospital from fire-related injuries.

The iconic MGM Grand opened its doors in 1973, serving as a testament to the film company's success and achievements. Named after the company's 1932 film *Grand Hotel*,[2] starring Greta Garbo, John Barrymore and Joan Crawford, this hotel was the largest on the Las Vegas Strip. However, it was a sad day in 1980 when flames engulfed the structure, causing many of the guests trapped inside the hotel to wander the halls today.

In 1986, MGM Resorts sold the property to Bally Manufacturing, which reopened the property as Bally's Las Vegas Hotel and Casino. Next, the MGM Grand was relocated to another building farther south on the Las Vegas Strip. Then, in 1995, Bally's was purchased by Hilton Hotels Corporation.

Since that tragic day in 1980, several guests and employees have reported strange occurrences throughout the building. Many have reported seeing ghostly figures roaming the hallways and stairwells. Guests and employees claim that these mysterious figures appear and quickly disappear moments later. One hotel employee claimed that a guest called the front desk, hysterical after seeing a pair of disembodied feet floating in her room.

Glowing people mover and porte cochere at Bally's. *Library of Congress*.

During the fire, several guests died in their sleep from the toxic smoke that engulfed the buildings. Rumors claim that several guests have spotted ghostly figures lying quietly on their beds as they enter the room. Could these be the apparitions of those who died in their sleep? Or are other spirits taking a break in a comfortable bed? Anything is possible.

Several people believe that the casino floor of Bally's is highly haunted, with several accounts of ghostly apparitions dashing through the area and then suddenly disappearing. The theory is that these apparitions are those of guests who died in the fire. However, they remain to roam where they once attempted to escape the burning building by running across the casino floor. Other theories suggest that these apparitions are the residual energy of those trying to escape the fire permanently imprinted on the hotel's casino floor.

The spirit of an older woman who appears in a puff of smoke from the cigarette she is holding haunts the casino floor. Then her dress seems to be covered in flames before she instantly vanishes.

Even though there are no reports of paranormal activity in the service elevator, many employees refuse to use it. Their refusal to take the elevator could be because several employees perished inside the service elevator

Bally's Casino. *Library of Congress*.

during the 1980 fire. Or it could be that they have experienced paranormal activity but do not want to share their stories for fear of being ridiculed or thought to be crazy.

The north tower's stairwell is another area of interest for paranormal researchers, as this is where several people were trapped and died during the fire. Several apparitions wander the stairwells, and sounds of disembodied cries, weepings, coughs and screams radiate from the stairwell and adjacent hallways.

The apparition of a small boy appears to many guests and employees on the seventeenth floor. Several people have seen this boy crying out desperately for his mother. When someone approaches, he disappears. Several feel that this is the spirit of a small boy who became separated from his mother during the fire.

Bally's staff and guests report several strange occurrences and disturbing events throughout the hotel. Other supernatural occurrences include smelling smoke on the upper guest room floors when no one is smoking nearby and sounds of disembodied screams believed to be those of the people who perished in the blaze.

2

CAESARS PALACE

The southern Nevada desert changed forever when Jay Samo opened the first themed resort in the Las Vegas area. Caesars Palace opened in August 1966, featuring elements from the Roman Empire. The venue started as a small, fourteen-story hotel with seven hundred rooms. Over the years, this themed resort has transformed into a small city, with six towers, four thousand rooms, a vast casino floor and a 636,000-square-foot shopping center.[3]

While the hotel rooms were still under construction, Samo opened the doors to the hotel on August 5, throwing a lavish, $1 million party. High-profile guests like Johnny Carson, Jimmy Hoffa and Vegas up-and-comer Steve Wynn attended the event.

In 1967, Evel Knievel convinced Samo to allow him to jump his motorcycle over the hotel's fountains. Unfortunately, his poor landing put Knievel in a coma for twenty-nine days and resulted in a crushed pelvis and femur. His son Robbie attempted the same jump in 1989 and was successful. Travis Pastrana also succeeded in this significant jump over the fountains at Caesars Palace in 2018.[4]

Frank Sinatra started performing at Caesars Palace in 1968 but suddenly pulled his act after the hotel sold one year later for $60 million to Stuart and Clifford Perlman. It is believed that an argument took place between Sinatra and the new casino manager, Sanford Waterman, who pulled a gun on Sinatra over a disagreement over Sinatra's $100,000-a-week salary. Sinatra would not return to the resort to perform until 1974.

Top: Caesars Palace. *Library of Congress.*

Bottom: Caesars Palace as seen from Paris Hotel and Casino. *Heather Leigh.*

Over the years, Caesars Palace has changed hands several times, including Hilton, ITT and Harrah's owners. Today, Caesars Entertainment Corp. owns the hotel, continuing with the vision Samo started in the 1960s.

Caesars Palace is no stranger to paranormal activity, playing host to several spirits that have decided to make themselves at home at the Strip's first themed resort. One of the most popular spirits at the resort is the one that lingers in the women's bathroom. While someone is using the restroom, the motion-sensor faucets activate when no one else is in the room. Additionally, sounds of tapping on the walls and stall doors can be heard by those using the facilities alone.

Additionally, a waitress on the graveyard shift experienced the phenomenon in this restroom and claimed that the running faucets would turn off when she put her hands under the running water. Turning on for no reason is not how the faucets were supposed to operate, and there was thought that it could have been faulty plumbing. But no one else experienced this activity, nor did it happen when others were in the restroom with the waitress.

Rumors throughout Las Vegas revolve around what is believed to be a cursed and haunted craps table at Caesars Palace. Legend claims that the casino lost an obscene amount of money on this table for thirteen straight months. Many believed it was a ghost helping gamblers win against the house. The table was eventually removed from the casino floor and destroyed.

3

CIRCUS CIRCUS

Many hotels and resorts along Las Vegas Boulevard have spooky stories and tales of eerie ghosts and supernatural occurrences. However, there is no hotel as haunted as Circus Circus, on the north side of the Las Vegas Strip. This popular classic casino provides guests with opportunities to shop, dine, gamble and enjoy entertainment at the indoor thrill park. With so much to do and experience, it is no wonder that some former guests may be overstaying their welcome at the hotel. This chapter looks at why Circus Circus is so famous and why the spirits may like to extend their stay.

On October 18, 1968, Circus Circus opened its doors and was considered the flagship property of Circus Circus Enterprises. Unfortunately, the hotel and casino were not close to the rest of the Las Vegas Strip hotels and casinos. Though high-stakes gamblers did not often visit, it was out of the way, making it a popular place for gangsters and mob members to conduct shady business practices. Plus, the many fun amenities and affordable prices made this hotel more suitable for families to visit while still experiencing a Sin City getaway.

The hotel has a history of troubling times, including financial issues, investigations for tax code violations and relationships with an organized crime family. However, these problematic incidents did not stop the hotel from completing expansions in 1980, 1986 and 1996. In addition, the hotel changed ownership many times to save it financially and possibly cover up mafia connections. Today, Circus Circus is owned by local real estate investor Phil Ruffin.

Circus Circus Casino sign. *Library of Congress.*

In addition to the financial troubles, ownership issues and other events that negatively affected Circus Circus, this hotel has been the site of many murders. For example, in a robbery gone bad ending in a double homicide, a Vietnamese couple was stabbed to death in their room.[5] The homicide is not the only murder in the hotel covered in this chapter.

With all of the drama and death Circus Circus has endured, it is no wonder that paranormal activity is attracted to this hotel. It is possible to experience ghostly encounters and strange occurrences in about every area of the hotel. For example, several guests have reported hearing strange noises in the hallway. When the guests look out, there is no one in sight. Others have listened to phantom noises in their room and, on further investigation, find no natural or explainable cause for the sound.

Back to the topic of homicides, one of the most notorious murders at the hotel occurred in Room 123, where the victims were a mother and son. Police reports determined that the mother had killed the son and then committed suicide. Rumors claim the spirits from the murder-suicide victims haunt the room and hallways nearby. Paranormal activity surrounding this incident includes hearing whispers of a young boy crying "Help me." When some guests go into the bathroom, the words *help me* are written on the mirror. One chilling encounter with these two spirits involved a guest who reported seeing a woman and her young child. They approached the guest, asking if they had seen a man named Robert, then they immediately disappeared. Some have speculated that Robert was the child's father. He may hold the key to what happened in Room 123. Additional reports of paranormal activity include furniture moving around the room and the apparition of a small boy leering at guests from the foot of the bed and in the hallway near the room.

Is the paranormal activity surrounding Room 123 the result of the murder-suicide that occurred in the room? Or could it be a manifestation of the many stories shared and urban legends that spawned as a result of this horrific incident? Though it is reported that this incident was a murder-suicide, there is still speculation as to what really happened in Room 123. Today, it is possible that the spirits and paranormal activity are a combination of the spirits haunting the room and the hallways of Circus Circus, but, because so many people have shared this story and the related hauntings, there could also be a bit of an egregore (thought form) happening here, too.

Other ghostly encounters at Circus Circus include paranormal activity in the poker rooms, central kitchen and several guest rooms throughout the hotel.[6] Several visitors have reported seeing the full-body apparitions of three men in the kitchen and hearing strange phantom noises in almost every part of the hotel.

It is unknown how many mob victims died in the vicinity of Circus Circus, but several believe Anthony John Spilotro was responsible for dozens of mob-related murders. Spilotro, nicknamed "Tony the Ant," belonged to the Chicago outfit of the American mobsters and was the leader of the Hole in the Wall Gang. He was in charge of the casino's gift shop, where he skimmed money from both the hotel and other mafia-owned casinos in the area. He was also a skilled assassin feared by many for his brutal killing style, including throwing people out of hotel windows. His greed got the best of him, and he was murdered on June 14, 1986, by his employees. His murder was just as gruesome and bloody as those of his victims.

Many of the ghosts spotted wandering Circus Circus could be the victims of Spilotro. Many have seen Spilotro's spirit on the casino floor, acting like he still runs the place.

In addition to the haunted Room 123, some of the other most-haunted rooms at Circus Circus are 203, 230 and 576, where reports have been made of strange noises, odd smells, objects moving around and apparitions darting through the room.

4

CORNER OF FLAMINGO AND KOVAL

THE DEATH OF TUPAC SHAKUR

The Corner of Flamingo and Koval in Las Vegas is an eerie place to visit, and those exploring might not want to visit this area at night. This creepy, dark corner in Sin City is where members of a rival gang gunned down hip-hop performer Tupac Shakur. However, several conspiracy theorists believe Shakur is alive and well, which is why there have been many sightings in Las Vegas of this rap legend. Whether the theorists are correct or not, several people claim to encounter the spirit of Shakur throughout the area and at popular places he visited when alive.

Born on June 16, 1971, Tupac Amaru Shakur grew up in a well-known family, many of whose members committed crimes against the government. In addition, many of his relatives were involved with the Black Panthers and the Black Liberation Army.[7] His relatives' work served as a foundation for many of 2Pac's most notable and memorable songs.

At age fifteen, he moved to Baltimore, Maryland, where he studied at the Baltimore School for the Arts, including courses in jazz, acting, ballet dancing and poetry. Though Shakur started as an actor, reciting Shakespeare at his high school, the world of rap music was calling his name. So, in 1988, Shakur and his family moved to Marin County, California, where he attended Tamalpais High School in Mill Valley. He actively participated in several drama productions and showed an exceptional talent for poetry and writing.

When Shakur started his rap career, he used the stage name MC New York and began recording songs in 1988. However, most of his work was unknown to mainstream audiences until he joined Digital Underground in 1990. The following year, he rebranded as 2Pac, and his debut album, *2Pacalypse Now*, was released. Though many of his songs and albums were considered controversial, he quickly became one of the most popular rappers, serving as an inspiration to many who came after him, including Eminem.

By 1993, 2Pac enjoyed immense fame and stardom, especially after putting together a hip-hop group, Thug Life. Unfortunately, this group released just one album, 1994's *Thug Life: Volume 1*. This album is believed to have set the bar for what was later referred to as "gangsta rap."

After serving nine months in prison, Shakur joined Death Row Records in 1995 and formed the hip-hop group Outlaw Immortalz. The album *All Eyez on Me* was his final solo album, released on February 13, 1996. During this time, after the release of the three-part album, it felt like Shakur was making a comeback. However, his comeback did not last as long as he or his fans had hoped.

Shakur often came to Las Vegas, and on September 7, 1996, he visited Sin City to celebrate his friend's birthday. While attending a boxing match, Shakur and Death Row Records CEO Suge Knight had an altercation with a gang member who previously had ties with the record company. A large brawl ensued in the lobby of the MGM Grand that later resulted in the death of Shakur at a stop light on the corner of Flamingo and Koval. A dark-colored SUV pulled up alongside Knight's BMW sedan, in which Shakur was a passenger. Occupants of the SUV fired several shots into the sedan.

Shakur was struck by two bullets, one of which entered one of his lungs. He was rushed to the University Medical Center of Southern Nevada, where he died from his injuries six days later. His murder remains unsolved to this day. Many conspiracy theories surround his death.[8] Some say he survived the attack, which is why many people claim to have seen the rapper in Las Vegas.

Many have reported seeing 2Pac's spirit walking down the sidewalk near the area where he was shot on Koval and Flamingo, wearing the bandana he was famous for, before disappearing into thin air.[9]

During a paranormal investigation in an undisclosed location on the Las Vegas Strip, paranormal researchers were not alone. Many have reported encountering Shakur's spirit in this location and experiencing strange activity in one specific room. During the investigation, as the team was leaving the room, one of the researchers said, "Boy, wouldn't it have been nice to have encountered Tupac while here?" With no experience or paranormal activity, the team moved to another room.

Later, an EVP was discovered when analyzing the evidence and reviewing a video taken during the investigation. (An EVP—electronic voice phenomenon—is a voice captured on audio or video not audible during an investigation.) The EVP appeared right after the researcher spoke. It said, "I'm right here." Was this the voice of Shakur? Or was it another spirit not wanting the research team to leave? Either way, as clear as the voice was, it sent shivers down the spines of the group members.

Tupac has been spotted by neighbors still enjoying time at his Las Vegas residence. Some neighbors have reported seeing him walking along his balcony, which expands across the entire front of his former home.

Shakur has also been spotted in several locations on the Las Vegas Strip, including at the MGM Grand Hotel and Casino and Madame Tussauds. So the question remains: Is Tupac Shakur still alive and doing well, or is it his ghost that people see in Las Vegas?

5

DELL H. ROBINSON JUNIOR HIGH SCHOOL

The Dell Robinson Junior High School has served students in grades six through eight and is considered one of the more notable schools in Nevada's education system. In addition to helping students, this school is home to many spooky specters and paranormal activity. Despite others dismissing the claims, several students, parents, teachers and faculty have experienced strange anomalies and paranormal activity while in the school at night.

Are these stories real? Or are they just some of the many urban legends reported in the Las Vegas area?

The school is east of downtown Las Vegas and has the highest minority enrollment of students than most schools in the Las Vegas area. The school has been nicknamed "Angels." It is unclear if this nickname is due to the many hauntings reported in the hallways or if there is another reason behind the nickname.

One reported paranormal activity is that of an unidentified janitor roaming the halls with blood on his hands. Why this apparition is haunting the school and why he has blood on his hands is unknown. In addition, some students report seeing the spirit of the janitor outside of school. Some students report that the spirit follows them home, several blocks from the school. While following the student, the spirit suddenly disappears when they reach the front yard of their home.

Students who attended church regularly claimed not to have been as affected by this lingering spirit as those who did not participate in church did. Nevertheless, many students who experienced interactions with the janitor spirit also experienced extreme nightmares that lasted for many weeks. Some believe this spirit was trying to send a message; however, the meaning of the message was unclear.

So, is the ghostly janitor a spirit lingering in the halls of Dell H. Robinson Junior High School? Or is it a manifestation of rumors of a bloody janitor haunting the school's halls? Or could it be an urban legend that has survived many years and is passed down from student to student through the years? To this day, it is unclear if the haunting is real or fake. As with any paranormal encounter, it is best to trust your instincts and be prepared for anything when visiting haunted locations.

Another strange occurrence several students have experienced is the spirit of the janitor coming to students in their dreams before they even start school at Dell H. Robinson. Several students have shared stories about their dreams the night or two after enrolling at the school. When sharing these stories with other students, they believe the same spirit lingers in the halls and follows students home.

In addition to seeing the bloody janitor, others have reported strange and unusual occurrences within the school. Reports of light anomalies, disembodied voices and feelings of being watched and being touched on the shoulder by an unseen entity come from students, faculty, staff, parents and visitors.

What exactly are the bloody ghosts that students are encountering, and why does it seem to leave alone those who regularly attend church? Some theories suggest that this spirit is a negative spirit or some demonic entity lurking in the halls, searching for its next victim. But many believe the spirit leaves alone those who attend church because God protects these students.

Since the story of the bloody janitor's ghost has been passed down from class to class at the school, it is also possible that this urban legend has self-manifested and is now a lingering egregore.

6

EL CORTEZ HOTEL & CASINO

The El Cortez Hotel & Casino offers travelers a classic Las Vegas experience, showing guests what life was like at the hotel back when it first opened in 1941. The vintage style and modern-day luxuries make staying at this hotel a unique experience in Sin City. The El Cortez Hotel & Casino is truly a blast from the past, which might be why many ghosts and spirits have decided to stick around well into the afterlife.

This hotel is the oldest continuously operating hotel and casino in Las Vegas and was the first major resort in the downtown area. In addition to having ties to mobsters Benjamin "Bugsy" Siegel and Meyer Lansky, El Cortez Hotel & Casino has a problematic past that continues to manifest as supernatural energy today.

In 1945, Siegel, Gus Greenbaum and Moe Sedway bought the El Cortez Hotel & Casino from the original owners for $600,000. Another highly connected Vegas organized crime world member, David Berman, represented Lansky's interest during this buyout.

From the beginning, the hotel owners were dedicated to offering guests the most authentic Vegas experience possible. They did everything possible to remain competitive in the increasingly popular gambling and resort industry in southern Nevada. As a result, the resort underwent significant renovations, which added four new stories to the hotel, a swimming pool, a nightclub and a barbershop. A grand reopening ceremony was held in 1952 after completion of all the renovations.

Historic El Cortez Hotel neon sign, Fremont Street. *Library of Congress.*

Jackie Gaughan, who eventually owned 25 percent of Las Vegas real estate with majority shares in many casinos and hotels, bought the El Cortez for $4 million in 1963. He owned the resort until 2008, renovating the hotel several times during his ownership, including the addition of Guest Tower II in 1980. In the years following the sale of the hotel, the resort expanded by purchasing the Ogden Hotel across the street and turning it into the luxurious El Cortez Cabana Suites.

The El Cortez Hotel & Casino continued its tradition of renovating and expanding to keep up with the competition in downtown Vegas but still maintained the vintage vibe from the 1940s.

Employees at the El Cortez have shared stories about seeing transparent, white, disembodied hands reaching out from the darkness in vacant rooms. Guests, especially those staying in the Cabana Suites, have reported hearing loud, repetitive knocks on the door. When guests open the door, no one is there.

Some guests have shared stories of a ghostly shadow appearing in the corner of their room. The figure just stands still and silent and vanishes when someone detects its presence.

Could the paranormal activity at the El Cortez Hotel & Casino echo the hotel's past connections with the mob? Could the likes of Siegel and Lansky be holding grudges, which has them sticking around the Vegas Valley, haunting their former hangouts? Of course, anything is possible, especially when the spirits tend to ignore the "Do not disturb" signs on the doors.

7
LA PALAZZA MANSION

The La Palazza Mansion has a dark past, demonstrating that the underground world of the mafia extended far beyond the Las Vegas Strip. This mansion is breathtakingly beautiful, but inside the impressive exterior is a history of lust, murder, mayhem and the mob. The sordid past of the estate is why the La Palazza Mansion is one of the most haunted locations in Las Vegas.

Built in 1959, the mansion has undergone many renovations throughout the years, most recently in October 2017. The Spanish-style mansion is rumored to have been owned by a local mob boss and was the site of many murders. It is believed that the many renovations were designed to create hidden passageways and rooms for murder, mayhem and torture at the hands of the mob. As a result, enemies, insubordinate gang members and others met an untimely death within the walls of the La Palazza Mansion.

Stories quickly spread through Sin City, and many feared they might not make it out alive when invited to the mansion. In some of the stories, someone who disagreed with the owner was dragged into a neighboring room and never seen or heard of again. Some visitors shared chilling visuals of blood-covered walls and a random drain on the floor in the middle of a room. This room was not a bathroom, and there was no logical explanation for the drain's existence.

The home has changed ownership throughout the years, with every new owner discovering that they purchased a property with existing residents. One couple bought the house and started experiencing ghostly encounters and paranormal experiences while hosting a dinner party with friends. During the party, guests saw a wine glass slide off the counter, crashing onto the floor. Some guests heard hissing noises, disembodied voices screaming obscenities and screams claiming, "You broke in here," and "Kill her," coming from a nearby room.[10]

Another of the home's residents claimed to have heard obscenities and sexual comments yelled at them when in the shower and feeling uneasy when inside the mansion. One resident reported being shoved while in the shower, almost causing her to lose her balance. Interestingly, those who do not believe in paranormal activity, including a previous owner, report hearing strange noises but describe these noises as more of a consistent buzzing or hum.

The most dangerous paranormal threat experienced by a former owner of the La Palazza Mansion was when glasses started falling off the wine rack. The owner pulled out a sword to challenge the entity. The spirit was probably feeling threatened or excited by the challenge, and it attacked the owner of the mansion. The owner started feeling an unseen force choking him, which is believed to be one of the angry spirits in the home.

One of the more popular spectral residents of La Palazza Mansion is an older woman wearing oversized sunglasses. This woman is not believed to have been murdered in the home and is often spotted sitting on the porch smoking cigarettes. Some paranormal researchers believe that she was the bookkeeper and money counter for the mob boss who owned the home. Others share rumors that she was the mob boss's relative, possibly his mother. Though many knew who she was, she kept to herself and often conducted her money-counting activities alone in the mansion's attic.

Though this woman is believed to have spent a lot of time alone, holed up in the attic, she was not as innocent as many think. Rumors have it that this woman was as nasty as the mob boss and known for drinking and smoking cigars with the boys. There are also suspicions that she played an integral part in the murder-room happenings, including luring men to the room and guarding the remains until they could be disposed of.

With so many strange reports, attacks from unseen forces and other paranormal accounts, it is no wonder that La Palazza Mansion is often called "Satan's Mansion."

8

LAS VEGAS ACADEMY OF THE ARTS

The haunted Las Vegas Academy of the Arts is located on South Seventh Street. The building was the first Las Vegas area high school, opening in 1931. It served the families settling in the area during the construction of the Hoover Dam. The art deco building was transformed into the Las Vegas Academy of the Arts in the early 1990s and has been graduating students ever since.

The Union Pacific Railroad deeded to the city the land where the main high school building was erected. The main building is the one location at the school that is most known for being haunted. Reports of paranormal activity go back to when the school was the Las Vegas High School.

The most famous of the spirits at the school is Mr. Petrie, an older gentleman wearing a suit and tie. He is often spotted in the performing arts center. Paranormal activity surrounding this spirit includes strange noises, icy cold drafts, misplaced items, flickering lights and slamming doors. There is a rumor that Mr. Petrie appeared in a school yearbook photo in 1968. It is unknown who Mr. Petrie was, but students and staff have affectionately named him and welcomed his presence. Some people believe he is a former teacher, especially since one woman was talking loudly in the school with friends and the finely dressed gentleman appeared, looking sternly at them and putting his finger to his lips to silence them.

Another legend surrounding the spirit of Mr. Petrie concerns an older man who died in a house fire on the school's property. There are reports that Frank Partie and his wife, Sylvia, lived on the property where the performing arts center stands today. However, his cause of death, in 1964 at the age of seventy-seven, is not known.[11]

Another strange occurrence at the Las Vegas Academy of the Arts is that of a phantom piano player. It is believed that the invisible pianist is Will Lowden, son of school benefactors Sue and Paul Lowden. Lowden, who died as a teenager, is believed to be playing the piano and behind strange noises and occurrences.

9
LAS VEGAS MOTOR SPEEDWAY

L as Vegas Motor Speedway (LVMS) is a popular destination for NASCAR fans nestled approximately fifteen miles northeast of the Strip. The complex has 1,200 acres of land housing multiple tracks for motorsports racing. LVMS is owned by Speedway Motorsports Inc. of Charlotte, North Carolina.[12] This famous Las Vegas attraction hosts several events throughout the year, including the Electric Daisy Carnival and the World of Outlaws. Additionally, the track was featured as the finish line for *The Amazing Race—Season 24*. The second most popular event for NASCAR fans is the Glittering Lights celebration, which features a drive-through holiday lights spectacular.

With so much activity, one would think there would be much paranormal activity at LVMS. But no reports of such activity are readily available, and no one has stepped forward to share stories of encountering ghosts of the track's past.

Despite the lack of reports of paranormal activity, the track has been home to several tragic incidents, including a man claiming that the spirit of a NASCAR racer told him to conduct several heinous acts.

One interesting story is that this man faced several charges, including attempted murder, DUI and battery with a deadly weapon. He also intentionally drove his car the wrong way on the 215 Beltway, causing a series of crashes. When asked by detectives why he did what he did, his answer was, "The ghost of Dale Earnhardt told me to."[13]

Cars line up before a race at Las Vegas Motor Speedway. *Heather Leigh.*

According to Fox5 Las Vegas, the fifty-one-year-old suspect appeared in court for a bond hearing, where he gave the supernatural explanation for his actions. So, did the ghost of Earnhardt, "The Intimidator," instruct the suspect to drive the wrong way? It is more likely that he was hearing voices

View of the entrance to the Glittering Lights display at Las Vegas Motor Speedway. *Heather Leigh.*

in his head as a result of heroin and methamphetamine in his system at the time. But at least he was creative and will forever be a part of the Vegas Valley's legends, lore, ghosts and other out-of-this-world stories.

LVMS has been the site of a few deaths, which makes the fact that there are no public reports of paranormal activity here fascinating. However, the report of a death—a murder and a dumped body—could be something to fuel paranormal activity at the track. The event was tragic enough, but still no reports of supernatural activity have been released or shared about LVMS.

On February 18, 2022, the body of a murder victim was found dumped just outside the gate on Las Vegas Boulevard and Checkered Flag Lane.[14] The *Las Vegas Review-Journal* reported that the Clark County coroner's office believed the forty-three-year-old man was killed elsewhere and dropped near LVMS.

Finally, the death of an IndyCar driver during the final race of the 2011 season leaves many paranormal researchers wondering why there have been no sightings of Indianapolis 500 winner and 2005 series champion

Dan Wheldon. On October 16, 2011, the race came to a screeching halt on lap eleven when fifteen cars were involved in a crash. Some cars became airborne, and others burst into flames. The other drivers were treated for injuries at nearby University Medical Center. Wheldon was pronounced dead on arrival.[15]

High energy levels and nearby deaths make LVMS a prime location for paranormal activity. It leaves one to wonder if any ghosts or spirits are lingering in the stands, cheering on their favorite racer. Or do spirits wander around, wondering what happened that killed them?

10

LIBERACE'S COLLECTION

Born Wladziu Valentino Liberace, Liberace was a Polish Italian performer who rose to fame as a musician in the 1950s. Liberace made several television appearances, including on *The Ed Sullivan Show*; had his own show, *The Liberace Show*, in 1952; and did some acting. He was a regular in the Las Vegas entertainment scene.

Liberace performed at venues such as the Las Vegas Hilton and several resorts in Lake Tahoe. While performing in Las Vegas, he developed his colorful and flamboyant appearance, wearing the sparkling outfits he was known for.

Liberace led a secret life until it was tragically cut short on February 4, 1987. His private physician in Las Vegas diagnosed him with AIDS in August 1985. Unfortunately, Liberace did not seek medical treatment for the condition. The condition, cytomegalovirus pneumonia resulting from AIDS, was kept secret until the day he died. Liberace died at the age of sixty-seven at his home in Palm Springs, California.[16]

Like many other entertainers who called Las Vegas home and stayed behind in the afterlife, Liberace remained behind to watch over his valued possessions. His legacy and spirit live on, surrounding the many places where his cars and possessions are on display. Many of Liberace's haunted activities occurred when his collection was displayed at the Liberace Museum on Eastern Tropicana Drive.

The original museum location closed on October 17, 2010, and his collection is now located at the Hollywood Cars Museum (Liberace Garage) and Thriller Villa, the former Las Vegas residence of Michael Jackson.[17]

Celebrities portrayed at Madame Tussaud's Wax Museum inside the Venetian Hotel include the flamboyant pianist Liberace. *Library of Congress.*

Some people have reported seeing shadow figures and apparitions resembling Liberace near his collection at Thriller Villa. It is sometimes challenging to keep up with where he is in the afterlife, because it seems as if the famous Vegas entertainer likes to go around checking on his collection, wherever it may be.

Museum workers and patrons reported seeing a shadowy figure in the parking lot. Many speculated that this was the spirit of Liberace; at the least, it had a striking resemblance to the famous entertainer.

A vehicle from Liberace's collection on display at the Hollywood Cars Museum. *Heather Leigh*.

Liberace owned a restaurant near the former museum location in Tivoli Gardens. He purchased the restaurant in 1982 and frequented it until he stopped making public appearances. After his death, the restaurant was renamed Carluccio's Tivoli Gardens, and the new owners kept Liberace's style and design for the Italian restaurant. An employee cleaning the restaurant noticed a reflection of what appeared to be a cape from the piano on display. However, nothing in the area resembled a cape or what he saw in the reflection.

Other reports of paranormal activity within Liberace's former restaurant include sounds of silverware and glasses clinking and clanking. On slower days, sounds of chatter, like a party, can be heard.

Some have even reported that Liberace still oversees restaurant operations from the afterlife and does not take kindly to criticism. A patron who said not-so-nice words about Liberace's flamboyant lifestyle experienced a large potted tree almost falling on him at the restaurant. The tree was so heavy that it took five men to replant it. So, when you are near where Liberace may haunt, it is best not to say anything negative about him, unless you want to feel his wrath.

Additional reports of Liberace's spirit are set around his former home, mainly hanging around his pool. One paranormal team captured the image of an apparition of a woman staring back at them from the kitchen.

Las Vegas is so glamorous and exciting that Liberace, dazzling entertainer that he was, returns time and time again for an encore. When visiting Hollywood Cars Museum or Tivoli Gardens, keep an eye out. You might be lucky enough to capture a glimpse of Liberace's ghost.

11

LITTLE CHOO CHOO DAYCARE

Once upon a time, there was a place in Las Vegas where parents took their children for a day of supervision, childhood innocence, education and fun. The Little Choo Choo Daycare was a popular place for parents to drop off their kids before heading off to work. Unfortunately, this location was a site of some of the city's most unfortunate and heinous events. These sad incidents are believed to have caused the paranormal activity at the location.

It is unknown exactly when the Little Choo Choo Daycare first opened, but it was believed to have been haunted by two apparitions. One spirit was rumored to belong to an unidentified Black woman who was often seen wandering the parking lot. Some people reported seeing her moments before she disappeared into thin air. It is believed the spirit could have been that of a teacher who might have committed suicide while working at the day care. However, the exact details surrounding this incident or the spirit remain unclear. The mere fact that there is little information about a possible suicide on the property leads one to believe that this is just an urban legend passed down from generation to generation to explain the unexplainable activity in the area.

Another report of paranormal activity comes from a resident who lived near the day care and would often see an apparition in the area from time to time. The ghost of a young boy was spotted on the playground, digging in the sand with a toy shovel. The spirit of this boy was seen during the day and at night. Who was this little boy? It is rumored that he was the spirit of a boy who had been run over by a toy train, The Little Choo Choo, and was crushed to death. This incident caused the day care to close abruptly and later fall into disrepair. The facility was torn down, and the location was a vacant lot for some time until it was transformed into Ryan Mechanical Inc.

With the demolition of the day care, it was almost as if it had never existed. Many who have walked by the property have experienced creepy sensations and the feeling of being followed. It is also rumored that the spirits of the little boy and the employee who supposedly died by suicide still roam the property.

There are no authenticated reports of paranormal activity, leading many to believe that these are urban legends for those looking for a chilling ghost story.

12
THE VENETIAN LAS VEGAS

C ombined, the Venetian Las Vegas, Palazzo Resort and Sands Expo Center make up the second-largest hotel in the world. This mega-hotel has more than four thousand rooms and three thousand suites. Being such a large section of real estate in Las Vegas, there is no question about the possibility of the site being haunted.

The Sands Hotel was closed when the owner faced money and legal issues, rumored to have resulted from mob activity. Some claim the former owner shut down his hotel when colleagues and other high-ranking members of the mob started getting whacked. He closed the doors and went into hiding.

Sheldon Adelson announced in April 1996 plans to create the largest resort on the Las Vegas Strip. It was nestled on the former Sands property, which was imploded to make way for the Venetian. The ground-breaking ceremony for the new resort took place on April 14, 1997.

Amid a flutter of white doves, sounding trumpets and singing gondoliers, the Venetian opened on May 3, 1999. At the time, it was the most expensive resort of its kind. It has undergone many renovations, upgrades and expansions since then.

The Venetian Las Vegas is owned by Vici Properties and is operated by Apollo Global Management.

Guests and employees have reported unexplained phenomena throughout the Venetian's history. Strange occurrences include late-night knocks when no one is at the door and creepy, disembodied whispers in the hallways.

The Venetian Hotel on the Strip. *Library of Congress.*

Additionally, several visitors have reported the apparition of a ghostly woman walking between their beds at night. The woman who appeared in several rooms on the sixth floor paced in the room and then pointed out the window before disappearing.

Chances are excellent that you will encounter someone who wants to share a spooky story about the Venetian, including urban legends about the deaths of construction workers during the development of the resort. Reports about construction work deaths vary; some claim only two persons died, and others cite seven deaths.

There is a story about a worker trapped between the walls and the foundation. Related stories about this incident claim he lived in the walls for several days, eventually dying of exhaustion and malnutrition.

Several paranormal claims, such as knocking on the walls and a moaning sound coming through the vents of rooms in the hotel, are said to be caused by the spirit of this trapped construction worker.

Other stories from guests and employees include sounds of disturbing and strange howling noises within the canals between the casino and the resort. Some guests have complained that the waters get a bit too choppy and suddenly calm out of nowhere. It is believed by many who visit the hotel or research the resort's dark past that the paranormal activity is mainly caused by former mobsters who are still looking for the next big payday.

Though guests have reported paranormal occurrences in rooms on the sixth floor and the hallways, the most active location at the Venetian Las Vegas is Madame Tussauds. It is rumored that Madame Tussauds is the most haunted location on the Las Vegas Strip.

Anyone who has visited Madame Tussauds, whether the Las Vegas location or others around the world, knows how creepy some of the wax figures appear. It could be the wax figures that watch you as you walk around or the spirits that linger in the museum. Still, many people, including employees at the Las Vegas location, have felt very uncomfortable inside the building.

An employee told one interesting story at Madame Tussauds about the spirit of a little old lady seen walking on the second floor toward the elevator. She was seen walking into the elevator to the first floor, but when the doors open, no one is there. Some believe that this spirit, wearing a long period dress and a bonnet, is Madame Tussaud herself watching over her new exhibits.

Other paranormal reports include hearing piano music or sounds as though someone is randomly hitting a key with a significant amount of

Celebrities cloned at Madame Tussauds Wax Museum inside the Venetian Hotel include the mobster Benjamin "Bugsy" Siegel, who built the Flamingo Hotel. *Library of Congress.*

force. In addition, several guests and employees have reported strange noises, voices and bangs on the stall doors in the women's bathroom.

The shooting of Tupac Shakur occurred near the hotel, and many people have reported hearing strange voices and experiencing the feeling of being watched near Shakur's wax figure at Madame Tussauds. In addition, some researchers have captured EVPs believed to be the late rapper speaking from the afterlife, keeping his memory alive.

The Copa Room was an entertainment nightclub at the Sands Hotel that hosted many famous acts, including Air Supply, Frankie Avalon, the Carpenters, Sammy Davis Jr., Jerry Lee Lewis and Red Skelton. This establishment was rumored to be a front for mob activity and was a popular hangout for many mob bosses. Some paranormal reports are believed to be the result of these mobsters, who would hang out at the Copa Room, causing trouble, fighting and grabbing the butts of the showgirls. Common paranormal reports at Madame Tussauds possibly related to the mob activity include feeling as though one has been punched in the stomach, having someone touch one's butt in the theater room and hearing obscenities yelled when no one else is around.

13

OLD MORMON FORT

T he Old Mormon Fort in downtown Las Vegas is home to the oldest building in the state of Nevada. Though this place is a famous museum and historical site for people to explore, it also gives off creepy feelings, including that of being watched or followed, as well as some strange noises.

What is the story behind this historic landmark in Nevada? The history of the Old Mormon Fort dates back more than 150 years.[18] The trickling, spring-fed creek that flows through the Las Vegas Valley made the area where the fort sits today an oasis for Mormon settlers in the desert.

Before the Mormons settled in the area, this site attracted Paiute, traders, migrants and gold-seekers passing through the area.

Recent archaeological digs revealed that the site was home to the Anasazi and Paiute, evidenced by the high concentration of pottery shards, arrowheads and stone tools. The tools resemble artifacts found at similar sites, with Anasazi and Paiute origins. This region was a popular stopping place and trading spot. Hence, it is possible that the items discovered were left behind by people who traded with these Native Americans, and it is just as likely these tribes lived in the Las Vegas Valley.

The Mormons settled in Salt Lake City in 1847 and spread west immediately after settling in Utah. With Mormons moving west in search of religious freedom and riches from the gold rush, Las Vegas became a popular stop for weary travelers.

Entrance to the Old Mormon Fort in Las Vegas, Nevada. *Heather Leigh.*

A historic building remains standing at the Old Mormon Fort in Las Vegas, Nevada. *Heather Leigh.*

Carriage display at the Old Mormon Fort in Las Vegas. *Heather Leigh.*

In June 1855, thirty Mormon settlers arrived in the meadow area of southern Nevada with the assistance of local Paiute and the Mormon mission leader President William Bringhurst. The settlers made their homes near the trickling creek and soon started constructing their fort.

The Mormon fort was made using adobe bricks and consisted of four walls, two bastions and a row of interior buildings. The portions of the original site remaining at the location today are the original eastern wall and southeast bastion.

Unfortunately, when crops started failing due to the dry, arid climate the Las Vegas Valley is known for, the settlers abandoned the location in March 1857.

Though the Mormon settlement was not successful, its history and legacy live on. The fort was named a historic landmark in Nevada and is now under the control of the Nevada State Parks system.

When exploring the fort, people experience an uneasy feeling, especially when stepping inside the one building that still stands near the center of the fort. Additionally, the energy near the fort's perimeter, where there are old stagecoaches and structures used to protect the fort and its residents, is so high that it can negatively affect some people, especially empaths and psychics.

14

OASIS MOTEL

Unfortunately, the Oasis Motel is not one of the most attractive places to stay in Las Vegas, nor is it in one of the best neighborhoods. However, paranormal enthusiasts enjoy the many urban legends, scary stories and reports of former guests who have overstayed their welcome.

The Oasis Motel was a popular and affordable place to stay for those just starting out living the Las Vegas lifestyle, but it was soon overrun with death, devastation and mayhem. Of course, the motel put up star seekers and up-and-coming gamblers; staying at the Oasis Motel was often paid for in blood.

Most of the paranormal activity seems to stem from Room 20. Several former guests have shared stories with the staff and locals about not feeling alone when trying to relax in that room. But with a history that dates to the early 1950s, the once-named Em-Le Motel was the home to countless criminal acts, including prostitution, sabotage, corruption and murder. The legality of things did not matter to many looking to strike it rich in Vegas, and most mob-related activities occurred in shady motels like the Oasis.

The location of this motel made it possible for it to blend in and be forgotten in the busy Vegas landscape. The hotel was nestled among popular and busy businesses in the city's business district near the Stratosphere Hotel and Casino, including pawn shops, bail bond offices, stores and tattoo parlors.

Two of the most mysterious and notable events at the Oasis Motel involved the deaths of two men who had no connection to each other.

Moreover, their deaths occurred months apart. Stu Ungar, a world-famous poker player, was found dead in Room 6,[19] and David Strickland, an up-and-coming actor, was found dead in the infamous Room 20.[20]

Like many gamblers and actors who became overwhelmed with their newfound celebrity status and wealth, both of these men's lives were cut short, and several conspiracies surrounded their deaths.

Like many gamblers in Las Vegas, Ungar had ties to the mob and was close friends with mob boss Victor Romano. Unger looked up to Romano, often saying he saw him as a mentor and father figure.

Ungar won two World Series of Poker championships (1980 and 1981). When he won his first tournament, he was the youngest player to win the championship, just twenty-seven.[21]

When Ungar finished ninth in the World Series of Poker championships on November 20, 1998, he was honored with a $25,000 prize, which was the highlight of his evening. Unfortunately, he was later found dead from a drug overdose in his room at the Oasis Motel. But not many people believed the overdose was the legitimate cause of his death.

Rumors spread through Sin City about Unger's financial difficulties and his owing hundreds of thousands of dollars for sports betting and drugs. Though on the night of his death there were not enough drugs in his system to induce an overdose, it was believed that his continued drug habits led to his death. Others believe Ungar might have owed the mob money and that they were responsible for his untimely death.

Regardless of how Ungar died, his passing caused a lot of chatter. Though his body was found in Room 6 of the motel, several paranormal researchers believe the strange occurrences throughout the motel might be tied to Ungar's passing. Perhaps he is seeking his killer.

Several months later, Strickland, a television and minor movie actor, was found dead in his room at the Oasis. Strickland was best known for playing Todd Stiles, a rock music reporter in the television series *Suddenly Susan*. He also had ongoing roles in hit television shows such as *Mad About You* and *Sister, Sister*.

Throughout his career, fellow actors and actresses reported that he struggled with drug and alcohol issues and suffered from bipolar disorder. He had stopped taking lithium, a medication used to control his bipolar disorder, just days before his death. While in Las Vegas, he was partying with fellow actor Andy Dick and checked into his hotel room. On March 22, 1999, he was found hanging in his room by a bed sheet.

Strickland's death was in Room 20, which is the room that seems to be the most active, paranormally speaking. Guests have reported seeing things move and strange anomalies and hearing voices and knocking on the door when no one is there.

In addition to the Oasis Motel being haunted by the spirits of former guests, the land surrounding it is also a hotbed of paranormal activity. Several people have reported strange and unexplained occurrences at and around the nearby Stratosphere, which is covered in a later chapter.

15

PLANET HOLLYWOOD HOTEL

Planet Hollywood is recognized worldwide, with millions of people visiting its restaurants and staying at its hotels annually. In Las Vegas, Planet Hollywood was once the Aladdin Hotel, home to the rumored Panorama Suite, also called the "Supernatural Suite." The suite was on the seventh floor and was reported to have been the most haunted room in the building.

Today, guests continue sharing reports of paranormal claims in and around the Supernatural Suite. The most common unexplained occurrence is hearing the room's door and lock jiggling as if someone is trying to get in. In addition, some guests have reported the room's door buzzer will ring at various times throughout their stay. But no one is found when the guest looks out the peephole and down the hallway.

Other paranormal claims include hearing whispers in the hallway outside the room. When staying in this room, do not leave anything lying around, because the spirits are mischievous. Items will disappear and turn up hours or days later in a different location within the suite. Nothing else has explicitly been identified, but many claim to feel uneasy and unsettled when staying in the room. Some have requested to change rooms, or they check out in the middle of the night.

A lot of the paranormal activity at Planet Hollywood could be residual energy from the long history of the property and surrounding land. Some former guests and residents may never have left Sin City.

Paris Casino and Aladdin Hotels, Las Vegas. *Library of Congress.*

Before Planet Hollywood was known as the Aladdin Hotel, the land was the site of a small hotel, the English Tallyho Motel, which opened in 1963.[22] This hotel was founded by the creator of the family game Yahtzee, Edwin Love, who wanted to provide Las Vegas visitors with a place to stay without an on-site casino. Though there was some success for the small hotel without a casino, travelers to Sin City wanted convenience and opted to stay at hotels with casino floors.

Aladdin's Lamp historic casino detail in the "Neon Boneyard," Las Vegas. *Library of Congress.*

Old motels and historic neon art, Las Vegas. *Library of Congress.*

The venue later reopened as the Aladdin Hotel on April 1, 1966, which remained for several decades. Then, on April 27, 1998, the original Aladdin was imploded to make way for the new and improved Aladdin Hotel, which reopened on August 18, 2000. The hotel changed hands and reopened on April 17, 2007, as Planet Hollywood Resort and Casino.

16

REDD FOXX'S HOME

Redd Foxx was born John Elroy Sanford on December 9, 1922, in St. Louis, Missouri, and he started his entertainment career in 1939.[23]

Foxx was a well-loved comedian and actor who starred in *Sanford and Son* in the 1970s, portraying Fred G. Sanford. He was also a regular performer on the Las Vegas Strip and eventually made Sin City his home, purchasing a house nearby. Much money went into reconstructing and updating his lavish home to fit his high-style and high-demand life.

Unfortunately, Foxx's lavish lifestyle was cut short when the IRS started an investigation into his finances.[24] The investigation was prompted when it was realized that Foxx allegedly owed more than $4 million in back taxes. The IRS seized his home and most of his possessions in 1989. Jesse Garron, a Vegas Elvis impersonator, purchased the house from the IRS in the early 1990s.

Two years later, in 1991, Foxx passed away from a heart attack while wrapping up a scene for an episode of *The Royal Family* with Della Reese. Since he was famously known for faking heart attacks, including during many scenes of *Sanford and Son*—his character would exclaim, "I'm coming to join ya, honey!"—everyone on the set thought he was goofing around and started laughing. Then Reese realized Foxx was not faking.

When Reese ran to his side, he spoke his final words to her, "Get my wife." At sixty-eight years old, Foxx was buried in Las Vegas' Palm Eastern Cemetery.

It is believed that Foxx's spirit has never left Vegas and haunts his former home, which is now the office of a local real estate firm. Both visitors and employees have reported spooky encounters, including slamming doors and lights turning on and off. In addition, some people have been lucky enough to catch a glimpse of Foxx looking out the front window of his former home.

When Garron owned the home, he and his uncle lived there for only a short time and left because of unexplained cold spots, ghostly apparitions and doors randomly opening and closing. Additionally, Garron experienced lights turning on and off without the switches moving up or down.

Garron could not find any reasonable or natural explanations for all the strange occurrences in his new home, so he enlisted the help of a medium. The medium felt that Foxx's spirit was lingering in the house and was angry because of the changes Garron and his uncle were making to his property. He was saddened by losing his beloved home and that a stranger was transforming it in a way Foxx disapproved of.

Foxx did not go away or slow down his ghostly interactions with the occupants of his former home. When the house was converted to a real estate office, he remained up to his old tricks. Employees claim he loves to play pranks on them.

During a paranormal investigation, several researchers smelled cigar smoke and coffee brewing in the home, which was believed to be part of Foxx's daily routine. These encounters could have been residual energy, but many claim to have various unexplained responses to questions asked, which means Foxx may be there, haunting his beloved home.

17

SAHARA AND SANDHILL

Sahara and Sandhill are where several paranormal events occur. But there are many possibilities for evidence contamination, due to open access from nearby neighborhoods as well as natural occurrences. In addition, much of the homeless population resides in the tunnels and nearby areas.

The most shared urban legend involving the tunnels near Sahara and Sandhill is that of an older woman who is seen driving a car and will chase people when driving on the nearby dirt road. When chased, if the driver makes their way back to the main street, the older woman turns around and disappears into thin air. However, if they continue on the back road, she continues to follow, attempting to guide people back to the main road. If she is unsuccessful, many claim that she keeps trying to run them off the road.

Other eerie claims reported at this location include disembodied voices and moans and wails from the tunnels. Some believe these are the sounds of people who have tragically passed away in the area. Others claim it is the souls of people taken by local demons. But the most likely natural explanation is that these sounds are naturally created by the wind blowing through the tunnels.[25]

More than three hundred people (primarily men) fighting their demons call the tunnels at Sahara and Sandhill home. Since 1960, thirty-one deaths caused by floods in Las Vegas have occurred within the tunnels.[26]

In most cases, when someone hears wails or howling caused by the wind or people living in the tunnels, the spookiness is enhanced by graffiti-covered walls, the darkness of the tunnels and the overall creepy feeling right out of an apocalyptic movie. Other reports of unexplainable activity include hearing footsteps when no one is around, but these could be the delayed echoes of the people walking through the tunnels.

So why are there many legends and beliefs that the tunnels at Sahara and Sandhill are haunted? Janice Oberding, another Haunted America series author, skeptically suggests that some of the legends in this area are attributed to the death of a couple involved in a nearby motorcycle accident. It is believed this couple now haunts the tunnels beneath Interstate 515.[27]

18

THE STRATOSPHERE TOWER HOTEL AND CASINO

Near the haunted Oasis Motel, previously mentioned in this book, the Stratosphere Hotel and Casino is one of the tallest buildings on the Las Vegas Strip. This structure stands 1,150 feet tall and has been the site of many paranormal occurrences. It was renamed on January 20, 2020, the Strat Hotel, Casino and SkyPod and is commonly referred to as "the Strat" by locals.

Five people jumped to their deaths at the Strat between 2000 and 2007; additional deaths occurred in 2014 and 2018 and the most recent on September 28, 2021. These people jumped from the observation deck at the top of the hotel's recognizable structure. It is unknown how these people were able to bypass security and get to the top of the observation deck before jumping.

Of the many deaths associated with jumping from the observation tower, some reports claim that persons jumped, others that they accidentally fell off the building. Urban legends share stories of those thrown from the tower.

Also reported have been deaths of guests riding on the Stratosphere Death–Sky Jump, a ride that opened in 2001. The most recent death on this ride was in 2016.

It is not known if the spirits of these people remain in and around the Strat's property, but they do add to the mystery of why this part of the Las Vegas Strip is one of the most active paranormal spots in the city.

Several guests staying at the Strat have reported eerie feelings and sensations of something creepy lurking in corners, no matter where they are in the hotel.

Stratosphere Casino. *Library of Congress.*

No one knows all the stories behind the deaths and paranormal activity at the Strat, which is why many urban legends surround this unique Sin City hotel. Several reports share conflicting information, including the number of deaths and how each person died when visiting the Strat.

19
EXCALIBUR CASINO HOTEL

The castle theme of Excalibur Casino Hotel lends a mysterious vibe to the atmosphere, which can add to the creepiness of the hotel. Some guests have reported that the hotel feels haunted; some claim the slots are cursed.

Excalibur Casino Hotel opened in 1990 and was a themed resort with a King Arthur motif. In 2005, MGM Resorts International took over the management of this famous family hotel on the southern tip of the Strip.

Left: Aerial view of Las Vegas, with a focus on the Excalibur Hotel and Casino's minarets. *Library of Congress*.

Opposite: The moon sits high above the Excalibur Hotel and Casino in Las Vegas. *Heather Leigh*.

Most paranormal stories surround the tenth floor, which is believed to be haunted. Guests and employees report hearing footsteps up and down the hallway when no one is there, and many feel that an unseen entity is following them. Other unexplained experiences include eerie feelings, whispering voices and heavy breathing on guests' necks while on the tenth floor of the hotel.

Some guests have reported that their rooms suddenly became cold on hot summer days when the air-conditioning was not turned on. Other paranormal claims have reported furniture in rooms moving independently. Strange electrical occurrences include guests hearing television static when the TV is not turned on, receiving phone calls with no one is on the other end and alarm clocks reportedly going off throughout the day and night.

One guest reported a dark entity in their room that seemed "haunted." Unfortunately, it was never revealed who this guest was or what room they were staying in.

20

THE FLAMINGO HOTEL
AND BUGSY SIEGEL'S MEMORIAL

If there is one hotel on the Las Vegas Strip that screams, "The mob was here," it is the Flamingo Hotel. Billy Wilkerson, who owned the *Hollywood Reporter* and several Los Angeles nightclubs, opened this hotel.

Like many men involved with the mob, Wilkerson was addicted to gambling. He traveled to Las Vegas many times, losing more money with each visit. To help accommodate and recoup some of his losses, his wife suggested he open a hotel. This way, when he lost, he lost money to himself.

During the planning process, Wilkerson brought on a few partners, including Benjamin "Bugsy" Siegel. The hotel officially opened the day after Christmas in 1946 and was named after Siegel's girlfriend, Virginia Hill.[28]

Siegel's ultimate dream was to create a lavish hotel empire influenced by Miami flair. Ultimately, his vision came to life when the Flamingo was born. Unfortunately, the hotel did not have the success Siegel wished for and ended up costing him and his mob financiers millions more than projected.

He wanted to create a gambling boom to help pay for his debts and to help prove to the mob bosses he was a contender in the Las Vegas mob scene.

Siegel was friends with Meyer Lansky, and together they created the criminal collective of Jewish mobsters called the Bugs and Meyer Gang. This gang was believed to have a subgroup of contract killers known as Murder Inc.

During his rise to mob stardom, Siegel also became good friends with mafia boss Charles "Lucky" Luciano, a hitman known for the disposal of many prominent New York mobsters.

Little did Siegel know that it would be Hill who tipped off mob bosses about his skimming off the top of the profits at the Flamingo. It did not take long for the mob to order a hit on Siegel after the informant shared the information.

Siegel believed his life was in danger, or he at least felt it would be, because of his management skills and skimming activities. He put all of his efforts into protecting his life. Despite the safeguards Siegel put in place to save his life, including installing bulletproof glass in his apartment at the Flamingo, mob assassins took him out en route to his home in Los Angeles. Siegel died from massive gunshot wounds on June 20, 1947.[29]

On the day of Siegel's death, he spoke with Allen Smiley, an associate, in Hill's Beverly Hills home, where there was little to no security to protect him. It was very convenient that Hill was out of the country, in Paris, at this time. The couple had a bitter fight on June 10, and she left to take a break from their relationship.

Was this fight and trip planned by Hill, knowing what would happen? Or was it just luck? After all, if she had been there, she too might have fallen victim to this horrific mob hit.

Moments after Siegel's death, Luciano's men stormed the hotel, claiming ownership and declaring Luciano was in charge of hotel operations.

Who killed Bugsy Siegel? To this day, the case remains unsolved. But with so many mob bosses upset about his actions and skimming, there is no lack of suspects.

Though the two had been friends from the beginning, Lansky did not hide his feelings about Siegel and is believed to be one of the many bosses behind Siegel's assassination. However, Lansky was not the only person upset or who held a grudge against Bugsy. Luciano was another lifelong friend who had ill feelings against Bugsy, especially when he learned of Siegel's inflating construction costs for the Flamingo and continued skimming off the profits. Precisely what was behind Siegel's untimely death is not known.

Luciano was also the mob boss who loaned Siegel the money to make the completion of the Flamingo possible. So there is an excellent chance that Luciano had ill feelings against Siegel and wanted him dead.

Since Siegel's death, the Flamingo has been plagued with new owners wanting to take control of the infamous hotel. Ownership has changed many times, including to the Hilton Company, which is now owned and operated by Caesars Entertainment.

Much of the remaining identifying structure of the original hotel was torn down in 1993. The new luxury hotel is home to lavish gardens, a flamingo habitat, a wedding chapel and a memorial to Bugsy Siegel.

The biggest question is, "Does Bugsy Siegel haunt the Flamingo?"

The answer is a big ol' "yes!" He does. Many refer to the Flamingo as "Bugsy's Last Haunt."

Some legends and paranormal stories involve Siegel, who is believed to remain behind in the afterlife to haunt two locations within the Flamingo Hotel's property. His spirit has been spotted in the Presidential Suite, also known as the "Bugsy Suite," which is believed to have the original gold faucets and bathroom fixtures from his apartment in the old hotel. In addition, Siegel has been seen near his memorial, where his apartment was located.

Some guests report seeing an apparition wearing a smoking jacket in the Presidential Suite. Since many of Siegel's possessions were relocated to the suite, paranormal investigators believe he is the apparition in the smoking jacket.

Some people have reported hearing disembodied voices around the pool table in some rooms. Siegel is believed to be complaining or sighing about his losses after resigning significant amounts of money belonging to the syndicate. It was a gamble that cost him his life.

One common question in Vegas is, "Why does Siegel stay behind when he can move on to a whole new world in the afterlife?" Some believe he has unfinished business and remains behind to find his killers.[30]

There is also the possibility that Siegel is not the spirit seen haunting the Flamingo. Instead, it could be anyone, including former guests, other mob bosses or even a demonic entity looking for new souls to corrupt.

If the ghostly apparition seen near his memorial is not Siegel, who could it be? And why are they attracted to the memorial? Could it be Hill coming out of guilt for what she had done? Could it be one of the bosses returning to gloat about their victory over Siegel after his death? As any paranormal researcher can explain, it is often almost impossible to know 100 percent what is haunting the Flamingo.

If it is Siegel haunting the Flamingo, all efforts to remove the hotel from mob activity and his association with its creation are falling short. However, Siegel does not want to give up his hold on his dream and will most likely continue to linger so he can see how his dream has turned into a reality and is not successful.

21
THE LUXOR HOTEL AND CASINO

The Luxor Hotel and Casino is one of the most iconic and talked-about hotels on the Las Vegas Strip. The Luxor, located across the street from Excalibur Hotel and Casino on the south end of the Strip, is a beloved hotel that was created from the desire in the 1990s to make Las Vegas a Disney-type destination and experience for families to enjoy activities, shows and more.

The Luxor Hotel and Casino is designed to resemble an ancient Egyptian pyramid, with a light beam shining into the sky from the apex. Some claim the hotel's theme contributes to the eerie feeling and creepiness behind the many mysterious hauntings and happenings there. Others feel that the theme of the hotel subjects the owners, staff and visitors to an ancient Egyptian curse that leads many down a dark path and several to their death.

The hotel is on the site of a former trailer park and took just eighteen months to complete. The structure comprises eleven acres of glass and has thirty stories, 2,500 rooms and 100,000 square feet of casino space. The light shining from the top of the pyramid can be spotted from space. It has a power of 42.3 billion candelas, and the temperature in the lamp room reaches three hundred degrees Fahrenheit.

In front of the Luxor stands a single sphinx, far more extensive than the one in Egypt. The size of the Vegas sphinx was determined to match the massive scale of the pyramid; the sphinx was built to stand 110 feet tall (which is 46 feet taller than the one in Egypt).

Left: The sphinx
stands guard
in front of the
Luxor Hotel.
Heather Leigh.

Below: Aerial view
showing the Luxor
Hotel Sphinx
and Pyramid, Las
Vegas, Nevada.
Library of Congress.

Unfortunately, when the hotel opened, it was not completed, and the CEO at the time, William Bennett of Circus Circus Enterprises, insisted on the early grand opening at the cost of the lives of others. The hotel's most significant challenge at its opening was the malfunctioning of the elevators, which were having trouble due to the hotel's thirty-degree slant.

In an attempt to rush construction, many things may have been overlooked, and this may have been a factor in the deaths of two construction workers. It is rumored that their deaths were covered up because the owners did not want the public to know about the incidents and wanted to protect the hotel's and the company's reputations. Little did people know that the shape and plans for the Luxor made the building dangerous and challenging to construct.

In several quiet, remote corners of the hotel, employees and guests have reported seeing the apparitions of the construction workers who died as a result of the hotel's complicated structure. In addition, some guests and employees have reported seeing ghosts roaming the tunnels of the hotel's Nile Riverboat ride, which is no longer operating.

Unfortunately, Luxor has continued to be the victim of numerous fights, disease outbreaks, fatal accidents, suicides and terrorist attacks. Many believe that these incidents are related to the hotel's curse and could fuel paranormal activity. Others have also felt that the structure of the pyramid funnels the energy, creating a negative force around the property and fueling paranormal activity and the negative behaviors among many who have stayed and visited the hotel.

The curse is also believed to come from the reproductions made to look like ancient Egyptian artifacts for the King Tut display. Plus, according to ancient Egyptian beliefs, the palace should have two sphinx sets to protect the pyramid adequately. That there is only one and that the hotel closely resembles a tomb has caused many who are superstitious to not enter the building, as they feel they will suffer bad luck if they do.[31]

The ongoing curses of murder, death, suicide and mayhem continued at the Luxor Hotel and Casino in September 1996, when a woman jumped to her death from the twenty-sixth floor. The woman's injuries were so severe that it was impossible to identify her, and she had no identification. Her body landed by the entrance to the buffet, which is now the location of the food court.

Since the woman had no identification and it was impossible for authorities to identify her, many conspiracy theories and urban legends developed. One of the most commonly passed around stories is that she was a sex worker recently diagnosed with HIV. In this theory, she committed suicide so she did

At the Luxor Hotel Casino, in a catacomb far below the resort, "wizards" entertain diners before a full-scale magic show. *Library of Congress.*

not have to deal with the disease and treatment. Another story claims that she was involved with the wrong people and was pushed over the railing on the twenty-sixth floor.

Regardless of how she died, it is reported that her spirit lingers on the twenty-sixth floor. Many paranormal researchers believe her soul is trapped in the place where she died.[32] Many believe she is the most active spirit to wander the halls of the Luxor Hotel and Casino and is most commonly seen on the twenty-sixth floor, but many believe she is the same spirit wanting the twelfth to fourteenth floors, where she is alleged to breathe down guests' necks. Some guests have even reported the sensation of being pushed by an unseen force.

The death of a man who fell from the tenth floor is another story that has created rumors and urban legends at the hotel. It has been ruled that the man's death was accidental and not a suicide.

Another significant event in the long list of tragedies at the Luxor Hotel and Casino is the bombing in the hotel's parking garage. In May 2007, a coffee cup was left on the vehicle belonging to a twenty-four-year-old food court employee. When the employee got off work, they spotted the cup. When they removed it from the top of their car, the cup exploded, killing the employee immediately.

Two men were arrested for creating a homemade bomb and placing it on the vehicle. They had no motive for what they did. Nor did the two men know the victim. It is believed that this incident was purely coincidental and that the employee was in the wrong place at the wrong time.[33]

In another incident, DeMario Reynolds, a former University of Nevada– Las Vegas football player, got into an altercation with Jason Sindelar, a mixed martial arts fighter. The room they were in was relatively quiet in terms of spiritual phenomena until that night in June 2010, when the dispute started. Sindelar and his girlfriend verbally fought each other at the party, and Reynolds attempted to intervene. According to one eyewitness, when Sindelar attempted to grab his girlfriend's neck and tried to hit her, Reynolds tried to restrain his friend using a bear hug on the bathroom floor.

When Reynolds let go and went into the main bedroom, Sindelar followed him, and the two continued to exchange punches. Finally, their fight was broken up and Sindelar left. But when he returned to the suite, he was attacked by Reynolds, who repeatedly struck him in the head and chest.

Someone at the party called security, but they came too late. Reynolds suffered from injuries related to being brutally beaten and was declared dead at the Desert Springs Hospital.[34]

There is no lack of horror stories coming from the Luxor, and the list of tragic events continues. In 2012, a Nellis Air Force Base airman was involved in an altercation with a colleague in the hotel lobby. As a result, the airman was pushed against the elevator door, which unexplainably opened. The airman fell twenty-five feet down the empty shaft. He was rushed to a local hospital and listed in critical condition. Unfortunately, he soon died from his injuries.[35]

There are also reports of Luxor being the site of a Legionella bacterial infection in 2012, which led to three guests becoming ill. Deadly bacteria were found in water samples, and the hotel promptly did everything possible to stop the disease in its tracks. But guests still became severely ill, even after the water supply was superheated and chlorinated.

After the discovery of Legionnaires'-infected guests, officials retested Luxor's water. This time, no signs of the bacteria showed up. Though the swift action of Luxor to decontaminate the water system may have removed traces of the bacteria, this discrepancy left the bacteria undetected, resulting in the death of a third guest.[36]

In addition to the spirits previously listed, five more ghosts are believed to be haunting the hotel. These spirits are those of mob victims buried on the hotel's site when it was a trailer park.

Other reported paranormal activity include:

- Room 30018 has a poltergeist, which is blamed for making metallic noises, rattling around the room in the early morning and making all kinds of sounds to get hotel guests to leave.
- The spirit of a deadly blond woman haunts rooms. She attacks victims by strangling them, causing many guests to wake up from a deep sleep gasping for air.
- Some guests have reported hearing fists hammering against their doors at night. When they check, no one is there, and when security checks the cameras, no one is visible.
- A shadowy figure appears in the periphery of a person's vision and will disappear as fast as it appears, especially when a person turns to look at the figure.

TITANIC EXHIBIT

Though not as haunted as the Branson, Missouri Titanic Museum Attraction, the Titanic Exhibit at the Luxor Hotel and Casino is home to many artifacts from the wreckage. This contributes to the many paranormal reports at this location. Artifacts from the RMS *Titanic* include luggage, floor tiles, windows from the verandah deck, ship's whistles and a 1900 vintage unopened bottle of champagne.

Several guests and employees experience strange paranormal activity, including seeing shadow people lurking in corners of the museum. In addition, some spirits keep reliving their final moments on the *Titanic*, which sank in the cold waters of the Atlantic on April 15, 1912.

Named after the Greek mythological character Titan, the *Titanic* was believed to be the ultimate ship and unsinkable. It carried 850 crew members and more than 2,000 passengers when it struck an iceberg, which pierced a hole in its hull. Less than three hours later, the *Titanic* sank to the bottom of the Atlantic, never completing its maiden voyage.

The Titanic Exhibit officially opened its doors at the Luxor Hotel and Casino on December 20, 2008,[37] featuring what is called "the big piece."

This is a part of the ship removed by divers more than thirty years ago. The piece measures twenty-six feet long and twelve feet wide and weighs about fifteen tons.[38] The exhibit is also home to replicas of the grand staircase, first-class suites and E Deck cabins.

In other reports of paranormal activity inside the *Titanic* attraction, guests have captured faint glimpses of apparitions, seen shadow figures dart from behind display cases and heard strange noises. Additionally, sounds of giggling, era-specific music and orchestral music can be heard, especially at night, when the exhibit is closed to the public.

Some believe that the activity results from many owners' attachments to their personal belongings. Others think residual energy was imprinted on the objects during the final moments of the ship's tragic sinking.

One legend coming from the exhibit in Las Vegas is that of the "Lady in Black," who is seen gracing the Grand Staircase, crying. Many believe this apparition is calling for her friend Margaret Brown, also known as the Unsinkable Molly Brown, who survived the sinking of the *Titanic*. The Lady in Black did not. Others have spotted Frederick Fleet, the *Titanic*'s lookout that night, standing over the Promenade Deck, attempting to correct his mistake of not seeing the iceberg in time.

22

THE MIRAGE

Like the Luxor, the Mirage is home to several tragic events and is the subject of many urban legends. One story that stands out is about when the casino was under construction and a wall fell on workers. One would think that this is not the best way to open a new hotel and casino in Sin City. Several employees believe that the workers referred to in this legend have never left the building.

One of the most commonly reported accounts of paranormal activity at the Mirage is within the bathrooms in the Terry Fator Theatre. These restrooms have a spirit, and people experience the faucets turning on by themselves. Some employees have also heard knocks on the wall; a member of the cleaning staff was too afraid to go in there. She instead would only walk by the bathrooms, catching the rosary beads in her pocket.

Another account is more of an urban legend than a ghost story. Still, it is chilling enough that paranormal activity may result from the tragedy, which involved the death of Roy Horn. The German duo of Siegfried and Roy, one of the most popular acts in Las Vegas, was hosted at the Mirage Resort and Casino. The show continued for thirteen years before Roy was injured in 2003 by one of their tigers, ending his entertainment career.

The most intriguing part of this legend is that many people believe that the original Roy had died and was replaced by an imposter. Journalists attempted to get to the bottom of the urban legend and requested a copy of the death certificate and verifications of Roy's death through the Clark

A view of the Monte Carlo Hotel, with the Mirage Hotel in the background. *Library of Congress*.

Roy Horn of the illusionist pair Siefgried and Roy with a friend onstage at the Mirage Hotel just months before Horn's career-disabling mauling by a white tiger. *Library of Congress*.

County medical examiner's office. Unfortunately, the claim was mysteriously denied, and this continued to fuel rumors, which spread like wildfire.

The legend of Roy's imposter remains in question today, leading many Las Vegas historians, enthusiasts and paranormal researchers to wonder if there is some truth to the story.

23

THE MOB MUSEUM

The Mob Museum stands on the site of a former courthouse in downtown Las Vegas and is a place where spirits roam and angry entities hide in the shadows.

The former Las Vegas Courthouse and the United States Post Office Building was erected in 1933 and features a classical revival style. In a drive through the downtown area, the beautiful building cannot be missed.[39]

The building operated as the courthouse and post office for twelve years; the next-closest judge was in Carson City. With all of the mob activity in Las Vegas, it was deemed best to build a courthouse there, as the judge in Carson City would make the four-hundred-mile trek just twice a year to hear cases in Sin City.

Now the site is home to the Mob Museum: The National Museum of Organized Crime and Law Enforcement. The unique museum is a must-see experience in the area.

Most spirits at the building are those of unhappy, convicted mobsters who all heard the verdict of their fate when the site was home to the courthouse.

One theory in paranormal research is that objects can contain the energy of spirits and possibly attract them to a location. Things, including personal items and memorabilia, can draw spirits to a site, allowing them to see their beloved possessions. Some spirits may stick around to protect their belongings, while others hang out waiting to see what happens.

Another theory is that when an object is in an area where a traumatic event has occurred, the thing may absorb the energy, almost like it is recording the event.

If these theories are true, and with so much crime-related memorabilia displayed at the museum, it is no wonder that the Mob Museum is considered one of the most haunted locations in the Vegas Valley.

So, who is haunting the museum? Many believe the spirits of mobsters and of local law enforcement officers who chased them haunt the museum.

One of the most exciting artifacts at the Mob Museum is the brick wall from the location of the St. Valentine's Day Massacre. Notably, many of the bricks from the wall at the site of this horrific event were located, transported to Las Vegas and assembled into the display it is today. During the events of that Valentine's Day morning in 1929, negative energy filled the air as seven people were gunned down by two men wearing police uniforms and carrying Thompson submachine guns. Five victims were from the North Side Gang; two other gang affiliates died in the gunfire.

At the time of the event, Al Capone was at his Florida home, but it is widely believed that he played a significant part in the incident, mostly because he wanted to remove Bugs Moran from leadership of the North Side Gang.

Since the events, the garage at 2122 North Clark Street in Chicago was demolished in 1967 and is now the location of a nursing home's parking garage. The bricks where the victims were shot were purchased by a Canadian businessman, who displayed them at various crime-related exhibits for many years.

The original owner, George Patey, sold many of the bricks; the remainder are on display at the Mob Museum. It is believed that more than seventy original massacre wall bricks are missing. The rest were donated to the museum by Patey's niece after his death on December 26, 2004.[40]

Several reports claim that those who possess the missing bricks experience significant lousy luck and that their bad luck disappears when they remove the bricks from their possession. Of course, not all owners of the massacre wall bricks claim to be plagued with bad luck. Still, some exciting stories make one wonder if the bricks absorbed the negative energy in the garage that day and are now affecting those who own, handle or come into contact with the bricks.

Some visitors to the Mob Museum claim that they feel an uncomfortable aura when getting near the brick wall. Several have mentioned that when they visit the museum, they either skip that display or avoid getting too close to the St. Valentine's Day Massacre brick wall.

Another unique artifact at the museum is the barber chair in which crime boss Albert Anastasia was murdered. The spirit of Anastasia might return to the chair, but there are also claims of negative energy surrounding the chair. Those who get too close start to feel a sense of dread and sadness.

Most paranormal claims at the Mob Museum are centered on the second floor, where the former courtroom was located. In this museum area, people have seen shadows darting around and full-bodied apparitions appearing and quickly disappearing. Many talk about their experiences in this area and claim it is not a happy environment.

Other reports of paranormal activity throughout the building include general claims of hearing disembodied voices, seeing shadows and being touched.

24

THE RIVIERA

With notorious connections to the Las Vegas Mafia, the Riviera Hotel is one of the oldest still-standing hotels and casinos on the Las Vegas Strip. Several mob-related murders occurred near the hotel, and this is believed to be causing much of the paranormal activity.

At one time in Sin City's history, the Riviera was one of the best hotels and casinos in the area. Liberace was one of the headliners at the hotel for many years. The hotel is a display of what a classic Las Vegas symbol is and has attracted attention worldwide for its service and style—and ghosts.

The Riviera Hotel and Casino, like many of the older hotels in Las Vegas, was believed to be haunted. However, many believe the stories of ghosts and paranormal activity are just myths. In contrast, other people firmly believe that this hotel was haunted because of their own experiences there.

Could these lingering spirits be that of William Nelson, also known as Willie Bioff? He was a mob informer who worked closely with Gus Greenbaum, a known mob affiliate who had ties to the Flamingo Hotel and Casino. Nelson was murdered in November 1955 after the mob bosses discovered that he was cooperating with the FedsCould his spirit still linger, keeping tabs on what is happening and keeping a watchful eye over illegal activity?

After coming out of retirement to manage and operate the Riviera Hotel and Casino, Greenbaum quickly fell into corruption, became addicted to drugs and developed a gambling problem. His corrupt activities led to the murder of him and his wife in their Phoenix, Arizona home in 1958.

The Riviera Hotel sign. The Riviera was the first high-rise resort in Las Vegas. *Library of Congress.*

Since the Riviera Hotel and Casino is where Greenbaum's life started its downward spiral, it is possible that he is hanging around the casino, hoping to change things or serving as a painful reminder of why he and his wife were murdered.

When cleaning the top-floor suites, hotel employees reported hearing voices in the stairwells and claiming to feel that they were not alone.[41] The presence in the top-floor suites gives off an eerie feeling, and many refer to it as the presence of something no longer living.

Some people claimed hearing voices in the stairwells, elevators and halls. In addition, workers have claimed to see apparitions of dead bodies lying on the top floors while doing maintenance. On investigation, the bodies disappeared.

One urban legend about this hotel involves the presence of supernatural creatures on the ninth floor. These beings would come out at night, wreaking havoc and causing mayhem throughout the hotel.

Unfortunately, there is no modern way to determine if these stories are true. The Riviera Hotel and Casino closed in May 2015 and was demolished to make room for the new Las Vegas Global Business District.

Most of the paranormal stories from this hotel are secondhand accounts, and no one speaks much about what happened at this hotel. It is a shame that the validity of these stories cannot be investigated and determined to be true or false.

25
TROPICANA

Nestled on the corner of Las Vegas Boulevard and Tropicana Avenue is the 1,600-plus-room Tropicana Hotel. This staple in Las Vegas history opened on April 4, 1957. The building seems quiet, but many previous guests have shared stories about the Tropicana being, without a doubt, haunted.

Many staff members deny paranormal activity within the hotel, but this is normal in Las Vegas. Few hotels and attractions want the public to know they have ghosts and spirits for fear of the loss of business.

Many paranormal problems reported in the Tropicana revolve around the hotel's lobby, where many feel uncomfortable and uneasy. Others experience strange feelings when they are near the giant tiki mask found at the hotel; people find they have strange purple marks where they touched the mask and capture eerie purple mists in photos. The big tiki mask gets blamed for many people experiencing bad luck during the days, weeks, months and years after they come in contact with the statue.

Many stories from the Tropicana have no standing and appear to be urban legends created to make visiting interesting. Still, one story shared by many paranormal researchers involves a guest staying at the hotel in February 2007.

According to the story, a woman was staying at the Tropicana with two of her friends in a room on the sixty-fourth floor. This woman stayed one extra day after her friends flew home in order to accompany another friend staying in a nearby hotel.

Slot machine arcade at the Tropicana Hotel and Casino. *Library of Congress.*

After this woman's friend flew home, she stayed alone in the hotel for one night. During this night alone, it was reported that she struggled to sleep because she felt that someone was in the room with her. She knew she was alone, but something made her feel uncomfortable and as though someone was watching her.

After she finally got to sleep, she was abruptly awakened during the night and saw a human male figure standing next to her bed. He was facing the wall with his back toward her. She screamed at the figure and turned on the light as the figure turned to look at her. But the man had completely disappeared when she clicked on the light. No one was there, and she was alone in her room.

She spent the rest of the night by the window with all the lights on and the curtains open. The following day, she left to check out and told a maid in the hallway her experience. The maid suggested she tell the front desk. The front desk clerk apologized and offered to extend her stay by comping the room one more night.

The eagerness to comp the room for one more night makes one wonder if this is a common occurrence and that the staff knew to do this when a paranormal complaint came in.

Since the woman refused to stay one more night in the hotel, she offered the room to her friend, whom she was going to fly back with. But he ended up having to stay an extra day in Vegas, and she gave him the room. It is believed that he also had difficulty sleeping in the room, but no confirmed reports or stories about his experiences are available.

So what lingers at the Tropicana? It could be anything from superstition surrounding the tiki mask to mob and paranormal activity tied to the land to former guests who want to extend their vacation into the afterlife.

26

UNDISCLOSED LAS VEGAS LOCATION

Many locations throughout the Las Vegas Valley prefer to remain anonymous when it comes to paranormal activity. These places do not let the public know about the activity within their walls. Anonymity is often the result of the business or venue not wanting tourists to know it is haunted for fear that people will not visit. In addition, some people still believe there is a stigma associated with paranormal activity and prefer to keep things hush.

This chapter shares the author's experiences at one undisclosed location in Las Vegas.

The site under discussion here is tranquil at night, and when the lights are turned off, it quickly transforms into an eerie environment. The creepy surroundings add to the suspenseful feeling when paranormal investigations are conducted in this building. But in one case, the spirits knew the team was ready and did not hold back when it came to making their presence known.

When the investigation started, three female and two male apparitions were seen pacing in the doorframe across the room from the investigators. The ghostly figures were dressed in traditional clothing of members of the Fundamentalist Church of Jesus Christ of Latter-day Saints (FLDS).

After some additional research, it was discovered that this area was known for having a heavy population of Mormon settlers escaping persecution in Utah. This information may explain why these apparitions chose to remain at a location where they felt comfortable and where they could establish a new life after leaving Utah.

Knowing that the FLDS settled in the area could also explain a recent interaction with spirits via the use of a spirit box. During a spirit box session at the location, one of the investigators asked, "Who is the current president?" and the team received a reply: "Jeffs." Immediately, the investigator corrected the spirit by saying that that is not the name of the current president and that there has not been a president by that last name.

However, if the spirits are of more recent FLDS members, they could believe that Rulon Jeffs, the leader of the FLDS from 1986 to 2002, was their president. The de facto leader after Rulon Jeffs was Warren Jeffs (2002–7). But his reign would have been too recent, because the building that stands there was erected in 1991.

Could the team have been speaking with someone from the FLDS? While it is possible, it seems implausible considering the times that Rulon and Warren Jeffs served as leaders of the FLDS community. The response of "Jeffs" on the spirit box could have been a miscommunication or even audio pareidolia.

Another fun experience took place when the author was investigating this location with her son. They were taking a break, and he needed to use the restroom. He went in and, after a few moments, peeked his head out of the bathroom.

"Hey, mom," he said.

"Yes," the author replied while standing at the opposite end of the hallway from the bathroom.

"There are strange sounds and knocking in the bathroom," he replied.

"Oh yeah," she calmly stated. "That is believed to be one of the most haunted locations in the building."

As soon as she said that, he quickly came running down the hallway, zipping up his pants. After that, he refused to go back in there.

The restrooms have been the subject of reports of strange sounds, disembodied voices and knocking on the stall doors when no one else was in the room. As a result, many paranormal researchers who have investigated this location have said that they will not go into the restrooms alone, no matter the time of day.

During another investigation, the paranormal team was in a room asking a series of questions during an EVP session. During the session, one investigator saw what appeared to be a large shadow behind a fellow investigator, waving its hand to gain attention. When the fellow investigator was asked if he was moving, he replied that he was standing still.

In the same area, in the background of the recording, there is a distinct growl. It was described as something you would expect to hear from a pterodactyl. The digital voice recorder was placed on a tabletop at least six feet from the nearest person, reducing the chance that the sound could have been someone's stomach growling. To this day, the team has no idea what the sound was or where it came from.

As may be apparent, this location is one of the author's favorite places to investigate, and it is a shame that she cannot share the site. But she did have a unique experience that sends shivers down her spine to this day.

The author has never been entirely convinced that the ovilus was a reliable piece of paranormal investigation equipment. That was, until one experience pushed her closer to believing in the validity of the device.

While investigating with a team, she wandered down a hallway, paying close attention to the screen of the ovilus. She was convinced that this small instrumental trans-communication (ITC) device was useless and would not provide valid, independent responses.

She didn't realize that she had walked just out of sight of the rest of the group. The previously silent and blank-screened ovilus started chirping.

Alone
Death
Demon
Devil
Sacrifice

The above words suddenly and rapidly appeared on the screen. She asked, "Who will be sacrificed?" A one-word response appeared on the device: "YOU."

When that word appeared on the screen, she immediately felt a finger touch her at the top of her spine near her neck and run down her back to her beltline. She immediately felt uncomfortable and turned around to discover that she was all alone. The other team members were around the corner, down the hall in the next room.

That was enough to convince her that the ovilus might be a reliable tool for paranormal investigations.

Many other paranormal experiences have been reported in this undisclosed location, including sounds of disembodied voices, names being called when no one is there, music playing with no explainable source and children's building blocks falling over.

During an attempted EVP session, one paranormal team even captured a harsh male voice yelling "F—— you" on a digital voice recorder. The same team also caught an EVP of a small child crying "Help me" in the same spot as the belligerent spirit.

This location is one the author and her team will never forget. But due to confidentiality contracts, she cannot reveal the site. Just know that she believes this location to be one of the most haunted in the Vegas Valley.

27

UNDISCLOSED
LAS VEGAS STRIP LOCATION

O ne more undisclosed location in Las Vegas is worth mentioning. This site is nestled right on the Strip and was known as a popular mob hangout back in the day. But then again, what wasn't a popular mob hangout?

This location is another that the author believes to be one of the most paranormally active in the Vegas Valley. After one evening of investigating this location, she had no doubt that former mob members continued in their activities as if they were still living and their victims were begging for closure.

When investigating this location, the author and other researchers had an exciting EVP session using a spirit box. The spirit seemed to be leading the team to a spot where its body may have been buried to hide the truth behind its murder.

The male voice kept talking through the spirit box, leading investigators to a specific location in the room.

Move left
Continue forward
Move back a bit
Go right
Stop! [the spirit suddenly yelled]
Body below

The Las Vegas Strip, looking down on the Bellagio Hotel's "dancing fountains'" show. *Library of Congress.*

The team tried to get more information, but the spirit they were communicating with suddenly stopped talking through the spirit box and seemed to have left the room. Was the spirit leading paranormal researchers to a location where its body was buried? Anything is possible. Further research revealed an urban legend that members of the mob murdered many people in this location. There is believed to be a body (if not more than one) remaining in the floor of this location.

Other familiar stories of paranormal activity at this location center on the bathroom. (Why are bathrooms always haunted?)

Several people, including guests and employees, have reported strange occurrences in the downstairs bathroom at this location. Common reports include the feeling of not being alone, rapping on the stall doors, banging on the walls and the sound of running water. Like many other locations where bathrooms are believed to be haunted, several employees refuse to go into the bathrooms alone.

Another exciting experience centered on the piano in the center of one of the rooms at this location. Researchers investigating the room heard a loud sound, as if one key was struck with a significant amount of force. It captured the attention of every investigator there that night. Later, when digital voice recorders were reviewed, the sound was captured, along with another striking of the piano keys. Someone, or something, was playing the piano while the team was investigating.

During the same investigation, one researcher started to act strangely near the piano and had to sit down on the bench to regain her composure. Suddenly, she stopped acting like herself and became melancholy. She could not describe how she was feeling, nor did she know why she was feeling that way.

Another investigator removed her from the location, and the woman suddenly started to return to normal. There was no reason for her to feel this way. Theories about what happened to her include spirits of mob victims trying to oppress her, influencing her actions and playing with her emotions.

The same evening, the author was walking through an area of this building with several other investigators conducting EVP and spirit box sessions. The paranormal team stopped in one room when they heard the voices of a male and a female arguing through the spirit box.

The investigators felt uncomfortable listening to their spirit conversation, but eventually, the spirits started responding to questions the investigators asked. A little bit into the conversation, the male voice told the female voice, "Shut your mouth." Immediately after, the author felt as if someone had punched her in the stomach.

Did the author experience what the female may have felt from the bullying of the male telling her to shut up? It is possible. The author may have experienced what someone felt during a fight or while influenced by a mobster.

One group of the paranormal team investigating this undisclosed location is believed to have been communicating with a cop who had worked against the mob. During this communication with the spirit, there were EVPs of a voice mentioning "courthouse," "conviction," "testify" and "murder."

The team captured an EVP in one of the rooms that said, "Freeze, police!" This EVP may have been associated with the spirit they were communicating with, or it could have been a residual haunting from a time when the mob-controlled location was raided by police.

A spirit box session led the investigators to believe the cop had died from a mysterious hit-and-run accident on the Las Vegas Strip. However, on further research, the team could find nothing about a police officer dying in a hit-and-run or any other evidence about the information they received during the spirit box and EVP sessions.

The team also had fun interacting with what they believed to be the spirit of a small girl at the location. The staff at the site reported seeing apparitions of a small female child playing around the elevator. It was not uncommon for the technology housed in this area to experience fluctuations and malfunctions while the spirit was spotted.

The girl would peek out from behind shelving in the area and be seen getting into the elevator when it opened.

One group communicated with the girl and told her to mess with another investigator on another floor. This group told the spirit the name of the other investigator and where he was. They also told her to follow him around and to play pranks on him because he loved goofing around.

At the end of the evening, when the team gathered to discuss what had happened, the other investigator talked about how what he believed to be a small girl was following him around and would not leave him alone. The other group laughed and explained what they did. When they shared stories about the night, it made sense that the girl's spirit was an intelligent haunting and that she was having some fun with the team while they were investigating.

Additionally, in the area where the girl was known to hang out, the author experienced something pulling on her shirt and tugging on her earring as she entered the elevator to leave for the evening. Was this the spirit asking her to stay? Or was it the spirit's way of saying goodbye and letting the author know she was still present?

Another fun experience the author had at this location occurred when the paranormal group was hanging out in a room, waiting for the others on the team to join them before packing up for the evening. The spirit box was still on, and the team was still recording. (You never know what can happen, even when the investigation is coming to a close.)

The author was standing in the room, speaking with another investigator, when she suddenly felt someone forcefully grab her butt. She stopped her conversation with the other investigator and called, "Who just grabbed my butt?"

No living person was behind her to do it, so it had to have been a spirit, especially since this area had been a popular bar with mobsters. Back in the day, it was not uncommon for them to grab the waitresses' butts.

After she inquired about who did it, a male voice came over the spirit box. "It was meeeee," the voice laughingly said.

Everyone in the group laughed, and it was a great way to end a night of stressful and intense investigation at what was believed to be a location where brutal mob activity took place.

28

WESTGATE LAS VEGAS RESORT & CASINO

Has Elvis left the building? Some people would say, "no."
Several urban legends and reports of paranormal activity lead many paranormal researchers to believe that Elvis still haunts Las Vegas.

Reports of paranormal activity include stories about Elvis's spirit haunting the halls of the Westgate Las Vegas Resort & Casino, formerly known as the Las Vegas Hilton. His spirit has also been reported hanging around the showroom where he once performed. Some people believe Elvis is behind the mysterious rattling of elevators as they swiftly travel between floors. The Las Vegas showman routinely traveled when returning to his room after his nightly performances.

At one point in Las Vegas' history, the Westgate Las Vegas Resort & Casino was the largest hotel in the area. It was a popular destination for tourists, performers, actors and artists, including the famous Elvis Presley.

This hotel, like many others in Sin City, suffered significant events, many tragic, including a fire believed to have been caused by Philip Bruce Cline on February 10, 1981. It is thought that the busboy was under the influence of drugs at the time of the fire, which started when a lobby elevator curtain caught on fire.

Unfortunately, the fire claimed the lives of 8 people and injured 350. Cline was sentenced to life in prison without parole.

Elvis, who is believed to be behind most of the paranormal activity at this hotel, performed more than 837 consecutive shows in the hotel's

International Theatre. Elvis was a headliner here for more than seven years. The King's final performance was in December 1976. He died several months later, in the summer of 1977.

One popular legend about Elvis's haunting of the International Theatre involves Wayne Newton performing with his band one night shortly after the King's passing. Newton and his crew created an "Elvis medley," and when Newton called for his band to start playing the tribute, Newton looked up to the balcony, where he saw a man walking onto it.

This theater area was supposed to be closed, and Newton claimed that he recognized the man as Elvis. He said that he looked right into the eyes of Elvis's spirit and that the entity smiled peacefully back. Newton said that this was a sign that Elvis approved of and enjoyed the medley Newton and his band created in honor of their fallen musical comrade.

Newton often said that this was his best experience.

Newton was not the only person to have a paranormal encounter with Elvis Presley. Other performers at the theater have reported seeing Elvis in the backstage elevator and near the green room. Several employees and visitors of the Westgate Las Vegas Resort & Casino have reported seeing an apparition resembling the King. In addition, several people have reported seeing him in the Tuscany Suite, where the Elvis Suite used to be.

Many who have stayed in the Tuscany Suite have reported feeling a presence in the room when they are alone, hearing music play in the room with no known source and seeing an apparition of Elvis in the suite.

So, why is Elvis still haunting the Westgate Las Vegas Resort & Casino? The most likely answer is that this is where he enjoyed spending time and that it had become one of his favorite places in Las Vegas. It is also possible that the many sightings of Elvis are the results of residual energy imprinted on the hotel's environment due to his energetic performances.

One story shared among paranormal researchers involves a guest who stayed at the Westgate with her two children and her sister. The identity of this person is unknown. It is believed that when she originally shared what happened, she wanted to remain anonymous.

After a full day of exploring the sites in Las Vegas, the group returned to their room to relax. While one of the women was showering, she saw what looked like a person's silhouette on the other side of the shower curtain.

At first, she thought it was her sister, so she ignored her and continued to shower. Suddenly, the water turned off. When she turned around to look at the water spout, she saw a hand slowly retract from the shower as if it had reached in and turned the water off.

The Elvis Museum includes exhibits with Elvis Presley's personal belongings. *Library of Congress.*

Spooked, she ripped the shower curtain open and realized she was alone in the bathroom. At first, she thought she may have imagined the hand. She turned the water back on and finished her shower.

The woman later discovered that her sister had gone for a walk in the hallway to help the kids burn off some energy. So, the woman was alone in the shower at the time of the incident. The two women did their best to hide their fear from the children for the remainder of the night.

Later in the evening, one of the kids asked, "Can ghosts hurt you?" Both women were shocked and asked why he would ask that question. The women were not prepared for his suggestion. He replied, "Because there is a man in the bathroom, but he disappeared. I think he's a ghost."

Immediately, the women packed the family up and moved to another hotel. The staff offered a free stay for the family in their room at the Westgate, but they refused and left.

Could these women and the child have seen one of the victims of the hotel's tragic fire? Or could it have been a wandering spirit making its presence known? Anything is possible, especially at a hotel like the Westgate Las Vegas Hotel & Casino, which suffered much tragedy and was the beloved venue of many performers.

29
WOLFPACK TATTOO SHOP

Quietly nestled on South Las Vegas Boulevard, not far from the Fremont Street Experience and Zak Bagans' The Haunted Museum and near the Arts District of Downtown Las Vegas is the world-famous Wolfpack Tattoo Shop.

This quaint tattoo shop is a throwback to old-fashioned tattoo parlors, when the Las Vegas Strip was starting to boom and the mob ruled the city. Wolfpack Tattoo Shop is no stranger to mob activity or paranormal occurrences.

The shop's address, 666 South Las Vegas Boulevard, does nothing to eliminate or reduce the eeriness surrounding the business. The number 666 is considered the number of the beast and is often used to refer to the devil.

Could the building's address have anything to do with the high levels of paranormal activity? Or could it be the fact that this building, like many others, witnessed more horrific events in a couple of decades than most buildings experience in a century?

According to legend, during the mob's heyday in Sin City, it created a torture chamber on Las Vegas Boulevard. That former site is now home to Wolfgang Tattoo Shop. The tattoo artists are often accompanied by spirits who have remained behind, seeking answers to what happened, causing the spirits' sudden demise.

Several people visiting and working at the tattoo shop have seen items come off the walls, heard crashes with no source and returned to the shop to find things broken. Several tools and objects have mysteriously disappeared and randomly reappeared out of place.

Paranormal researchers have claimed to experience various paranormal activities at Wolfgang Tattoo Shop, including being physically thrown, scratched and punched by unseen spirits.

Several paranormal events at this location are believed to be connected to mob activity, especially since it is thought that the site was formerly a place where people who spoke out against the mob or disobeyed its rules were brought for punishment.

30

ZAK BAGANS'
THE HAUNTED MUSEUM

Zak Bagans, star of the Travel Channel's *Ghost Adventures*, is from the Las Vegas area. So it was natural that he chose Sin City as the home for his haunted museum. The site of the museum is believed to be haunted and to contain many haunted and creepy items. These may help fuel the paranormal activity.

The Haunted Museum is believed to be home to hundreds of cursed and possessed objects collected from all over the world. Zak's museum dreams became a reality when the doors to the venue opened to the public in September 2017, after Zak and his crew filmed several episodes of *Deadly Possessions* for the Travel Channel starting in April 2016.

The eleven-thousand-square-foot property was the backdrop for the show, which featured some of the most haunted objects in the world, including Robert the Doll and Charles Manson's television.[42] The museum's collection has grown and now includes a mix of haunted objects, items formerly owned by serial killers and movie props.

The building the museum is located in was built in 1938, and there are several rumors that the owner, Cyril Wengert, would perform rituals in the basement. This may have led to the paranormal activity in the building long before any of the haunted items were carried over the threshold.

It is also rumored that dark magick rituals continued to be performed in the museum's basement in the 1970s.

There have been reports of the first owner of the building terrorizing people and performing dark rituals in the basement, but these have not been proven. But Zak, employees and guests have seen what appears to be a black-hooded figure walking through closed doors. Some people believe this shadow figure is the spirit of one of the 1970s cultists; others believe it is attached to an object in the museum.

Several staff members have reported strange occurrences, including seeing unexplainable things happen during their shifts. In addition, several guests over the years have claimed to feel dizzy, faint, experience nose bleeds and have feelings of unease when touring the museum.

BELA LUGOSI'S MIRROR

Romanian-born Bela Lugosi was an actor in many horror films between 1931 and 1956. He portrayed Count Dracula in the 1931 version of the story. When Lugosi died on August 16, 1956, he was buried in a replica of his famous Dracula cape, while the original was left to his son.[43] The cape and other memorabilia, including a mirror, have been purchased and auctioned off multiple times.

Reports of paranormal activity surrounding this mirror started with Lugosi, who claimed that a black shadow surrounded people who looked in the mirror. Though he was known to play tricks with people's minds, several people who attempted to stare into the mirror's void collapsed.

A former owner of the mirror claimed that her uncle, Frank Saletri, an attorney and B-movie producer, was brutally murdered in the presence of the mirror in 1982. She believed he was murdered by a friend or someone he knew, because there were no signs of forced entry or robbery.

It is believed that the mirror absorbed the energy from the murder and is the cause of a lot of paranormal activity that affected her life. After her uncle's death, she acquired the mirror, and immediately her daughter started being negatively affected. She claimed her daughter would feel bites on the neck and when she went to look in the mirror would see a dark entity inside of it. The daughter also suffered extreme nightmares of being attacked by this entity and would wake up with scratches all over her body.

Lugosi was also known for dabbling in the occult and would perform rituals in the same room as the mirror, often incorporating the mirror into the rituals. For example, he would practice his clairvoyance skills by looking into an inanimate object, such as a crystal ball or mirror, to conjure messages from spirits.

Lugosi's mirror was donated to the museum. Shortly after, the basement flooded. After investigating the flooding, Zak recorded bangs and rattling in the basement. Could this be caused by the mirror or just a mechanical malfunction in the basement? No one is certain, but it is an exciting story.

Zak witnessed a ball of light appear across the room from the mirror, traveled across the room and disappear as it entered the mirror.

Today, the mirror is set behind a curtain, and visitors must consent to look into it.

CHARLES MANSON'S CREMATED ASHES

In the late 1960s and early '70s, the Manson Family, led by Charles Manson, was a cult, commune and gang activity in California. Some members of the group committed murders at four locations in the late summer of 1969, including the murder of Sharon Tate, the wife of director Roman Polanski. She was eight and a half months pregnant at the time of her murder.

Manson and his "family" members were convicted of murder in 1971 and sentenced to life in prison without the possibility of parole. He served his sentence at the California State Prison in Corcoran until his death at eighty-three in 2017.[44]

Manson's body was cremated, and several followers took portions of his ashes. The ashes were kept as souvenirs. An artist, Ryan Almighty, created a series of paintings, Ryan Almighty Blood Paintings of Manson, using Manson's created remains to fill in the eyes of his portraits.

One of the paintings is on display at the museum, along with Manson's television, one of his prison-worn outfits, his dentures and additional cremated remains of the infamous cult leader.

DR. KEVORKIAN'S VOLKSWAGEN DEATH VAN

Jack Kevorkian, also known as Doctor Death, was an American pathologist who advocated for a terminal patient's right to die by physician-assisted suicide. He firmly believed that death was not a crime and pushed colleagues to help him introduce elective euthanasia to the world.

During his career, Kevorkian confessed to assisting more than 130 patients in ending their lives. His confession and other evidence led to his conviction for murder in 1999.[45] The trial focused on the voluntary euthanasia Kevorkian administered to Thomas Youlk, a man with Lou Gehrig's disease (ALS).

Kevorkian used a Volkswagen van to conduct his "medicides." It was equipped with a small bed and was the location where his patients took their final breaths. The feeling around the van is of complete sadness and hopelessness, leaving many who see it speechless.

After serving eight years in prison, Dr. Kevorkian was back on the streets, and there were rumors that he never stopped receiving support from the families of the people he helped. During his final years, Kevorkian gave lectures and interviews about euthanasia.

He died at the age of eighty-four in 2011.

The van is now on display at the museum. Many people explain that seeing it is difficult, because they could feel energy emanating from the vehicle. Several strange occurrences have been reported that involve this display, including strange light anomalies and hearing voices and cries coming from within the van.

Though the Volkswagen is not as haunted as the other objects in the museum, it sure does have a very haunted history.

THE DYBBUK BOX

The museum is home to what is often referred to as the most haunted object in the world, the Dybbuk Box. What is the Dybbuk Box? It is a box believed to house a ghost inside.

According to Jewish mythology, a dybbuk is a restless and malicious spirit often known to possess the living. The box was created to capture and house this evil spirit. In fact, one has found its way to the museum.

This particular Dybbuk Box has a unique history of ownership. Before making its way to Las Vegas, it was purchased in 2001 in an estate sale. The box had belonged to a Holocaust survivor, Havaleh, from Poland. Haveleh bought the box in Spain before immigrating to the United States.

When it was discovered that the box was a family heirloom, Kevin Mannis, the estate sale purchaser, attempted to return the box to the family, but they refused. They no longer wanted to own the box and suggested it never be opened because of the powerful dybbuk housed inside.

Unfortunately, the new owner of the box could not resist temptation and opened the box, which contained two 1920s pennies, a lock of brown hair and a lock of blond hair. The box also had a small statue, a dried rosebud, a small candleholder and a wine goblet. After opening the box, the owner started suffering horrific nightmares. He gave the box to his mother as a gift. Unfortunately, the same day he gave the Dybbuk Box to her, she suffered a stroke.

Since then, all owners of the box have reported smelling cat urine and jasmine flowers. Their nightmares are filled with images of an old hag who frequently haunts them in their sleep.

The box was then put up for auction on eBay, where it was purchased by Jason Haxton, who also suffered significant troubles after taking ownership. He and his wife developed blisters and welts on their bodies and claimed to experience bleeding from the eyes. They continued to experience these unexplainable ailments until Haxton managed to reseal the Dybbuk Box, keeping it hidden from the rest of the world.

After owning the box and publishing a book about his experiences, Haxton eventually donated the evil box to the Haunted Museum.

Is the story about the Dybbuk Box true? Rumors on the internet include a report from many years ago that the original owner, Mannis, made the entire story up and confessed that the box was just a wine box he had from the 1960s.

Could the made-up story have led to a self-manifestation of the paranormal experiences suffered by Haxton and his wife? Or were they in on the false accusations?

Whether the story is true or false or the result of a thought form, rapper Post Malone claimed to have been cursed by what he believes to be the most haunted object in Zak's museum. Malone shared that he suffered from horrible luck for several weeks after facing the Dybbuk Box.[46]

A series of unfortunate events followed him, including a tire blowing out on his plane during takeoff. The aircraft was immediately forced to make an emergency landing. Then, one month later, he was involved in a high-speed car crash. This was followed by burglars breaking into his home.

Several reports of strange activity have been reported around the box, including people seeing a black-cloaked figure that tends to linger and hover around the box. Others experienced strange feelings when near the box and the sensation of being followed when leaving the room it is stored in.

ED GEIN'S CAULDRON

Ed Gein, also known as the "Butcher of Plainfield" and the "Plainfield Ghoul," was a serial killer and graverobber who used a cauldron to boil body parts. It is not known if Gein was a cannibal, because he never admitted it. But those close to him suspected that he was.[47]

His body-snatching fascination led him to dig up corpses and use the skin to make the furniture in his home. When he was arrested in November 1957, police found various ghostly and morbid items in his home. They also found the bodies of numerous missing women. They had been killed and dismembered and were hanging from the ceiling by their ankles.

Police also found human skulls, household items made from human flesh and the cauldron believed to be used for Gein's morbid acts.

Gein was put on trial in 1968 after being deemed fit to participate in his defense. He was found guilty of murder, but it was determined that he was insane at the time of the murders. Gein was sent to Mendota Mental Health Institute in Madison, Wisconsin, until his death at the age of seventy-seven on July 26, 1984.

Gein's cauldron is now on display at the museum and is believed to have dark energy attached to it. As a result, some people close to the item feel a sense of uneasiness, dizziness and anxiety.

PEGGY THE DOLL

Peggy the Doll has a history of wreaking havoc among those who challenge her. Therefore, guests of the museum are encouraged to treat Peggy with respect in order to reduce the opportunities for the doll to affect them negatively.

Peggy may look innocent on the outside, but don't let this fool you. It is rumored that this doll is possessed by an impish spirit believed to cause debilitating headaches, chest pains and extreme nausea in people who come in contact with it. Some people have claimed that when they look at Peggy, they have visions of a mental institute. She is blamed for at least one heart attack. Some claim that merely looking at her causes pain and suffering in their lives.

Another theory about who possesses Peggy the Doll is that a woman born in London in 1946 might be the source of the activity. It is reported that this woman died of a chest condition thought to be asthma.[48]

Today, Peggy the Doll resides at Zak's museum, where she has her room. A spirit box is hooked up in the room, allowing daring guests to interact with the doll. Some guests have successfully communicated with her, even hearing their names called out and receiving intelligent responses to questions asked.

STAIRWAY TO HELL

Zak created a documentary about the Demon House in Gary, Indiana, several years back. The story behind this haunted or even possessed home inspired Zak to buy the home, sight unseen, so he could learn more and conduct some research into why the house was haunted.

The story behind the Demon House starts with a mother claiming that her three children were possessed by demons that lived in their home. The family reported swarms of large black flies in the house, the sounds of footsteps in the basement and doors opening and closing on their own.

The family brought a couple of exterminators in the home. They determined that there was no reason for the flies to be present. However, immediately after the exterminators left, the flies returned.

Strange occurrences continued, leading the family to believe that the three children were possessed. Abnormal activity included eyes bulging, a change in their voices and twisted-looking faces.

One day, the nine-year-old boy shared details of what it was like to be killed and was witnessed walking up the wall in the presence of a mental-health specialist and a caseworker. The seven-year-old boy started choking his brother, and it took two adults to pry his clenched hands from around the brother's neck.

Some people, including guests, felt that they were choking and nauseous in the home.

All the children received mental-health counseling, which determined that they were of sound mind and body. So, what was causing them to act so strangely? Many believe negative forces in the home affected how they acted and reacted to various situations.

Before bulldozing the home to the ground, Zak pulled out the home's staircase, below which objects were found buried in the dirt. He transported the stairs back to Las Vegas to be the newest exhibit in his museum, resting in a quiet corner of the museum in a pile of dirt the staircase rested in from home.

Rumors claim that the construction workers installing the staircase in the museum walked off the job and refused to return to the location. As a result, visitors at the museum feel faint and nauseous when near the exhibit, even if they do not know the history behind the Demon's Staircase.

Zak ordered the home to be demolished in 2014, and the staircase to the basement sits in the museum.[49]

Ted Bundy's Glasses

Ted Bundy kidnapped, raped and killed more than thirty women in seven states between 1974 and 1978. The exact number of women he killed is unknown, as he confessed to only thirty. He was finally arrested on August 16, 1975, for the first time and was released, because the police did not have substantial evidence connecting him to the murders.

Bundy was arrested again several months later for another kidnapping and assault. He escaped custody during transport from Utah to Colorado but was recaptured within the week. He managed to escape a second time, on December 30, 1977; this time, he found his way to Florida without being taken back into custody. He killed six more people during his freedom, including five Florida State University students.

Bundy was pulled over for a traffic violation on February 15, 1978, and was taken into custody. He was convicted and sentenced to death by electric chair. He died on January 24, 1989, at the Florida State Prison.[50]

The Volkswagen that Bundy drove during his killing spree is now on display at the Alcatraz East Crime Museum. The glasses he reportedly wore as a disguise are on display at the Haunted Museum.

More Haunted Items

Several other supposedly haunted items are found at the Haunted Museum, including Wyatt Earp's Bible set by a rocking chair reserved for this Old West icon. In addition, the funeral parlor room is decorated with hand-painted stained-glass windows from the 1800s. An abundance of haunted and creepy dolls and clowns are scattered throughout the museum.

Also on display are paintings done by serial killer John Wayne Gacy and artifacts owned by Richard Ramirez.

Contrary to popular belief, the Haunted Museum in Las Vegas is not home to Robert the Doll or Annabelle. Instead, Robert the Doll is safely kept and cared for at the East Martello Museum in Key West, Florida. Annabelle continues to be managed by members of Ed and Lorraine Warren's family.

31

SUNSET PARK

S unset Park in Las Vegas is visited by thousands of people each year who come to enjoy themselves and attend festivals and events hosted at the park. But many visitors are unaware of what lies beneath the grassy fields and play areas here.

Traveling along Eastern Avenue in Las Vegas takes you to Sunset Park, where legend claims that more than two hundred bodies were left in the ground when the public recreation area was built in the 1950s. It is a bit creepy, because many people, including the author, have spent countless hours enjoying time with family, exploring, relaxing and playing at this popular park.

Where did the two hundred bodies believed to be buried under Sunset Park come from? Rumors run rampant about this, many centering on the belief that the land used to develop Sunset Park was originally a cemetery. It is unknown how many people were buried there, but the number is believed to be between two hundred and two thousand.

There is a wide range of rumors claiming there are bodies buried on the property, but regardless of the legends, construction crews came and started construction for the famous family park.

Long before the area now known as Sunset Park was possibly used as a cemetery, it was the site of Paiute habitation, trading and exploration one thousand years ago. Though the Paiutes left traces of their existence in the Vegas Valley, they did not fully settle in the area. Reports claim that the land held no ceremonial significance for them.

It was not until 1909 that the first modern-day settlement was begun, when John F. Miller bought the land and turned it into a ranch. The Miller Ranch was very successful, and Miller was able to build Hotel Nevada, one of the first Las Vegas casinos. He eventually hired Bert Gibbs, who worked the ranch and lived on the site with his wife by his side.[51]

Research has determined that it is doubtful that the urban legend regarding the land under Sunset Park having been a cemetery is true, as the property's history does not include any specific plans to make it one.

It has changed hands in the years since Miller owned the ranch, including to J. Kell Houssels Sr., who purchased the ranch in 1939. Houssels also owned the Las Vegas Club and Casino. He turned the ranch into the Vegas Stock Farm, which bred and raised Thoroughbred horses.

After Houssels could not get approval to turn his farm into a golf resort, he sold it in 1963 to Wilbur Clark, the owner of the Desert Inn Casino. During the time of Clark's ownership, it is unclear what he and his investors planned to do, but a cemetery was not among the plans. This makes it doubtful that this urban legend is true.

The property and structures were left abandoned. Mary Gravelle Habbart, a neighboring rancher, tried her best to protect the land from destruction and vandalism. Clark County eventually purchased the land in 1967, turning it into Las Vegas's first city park.

If there is no evidence that the land under Sunset Park was a former cemetery, where does the urban legend come from? The answer isn't clear, but some believe the confusion comes from the North Las Vegas Cemetery, "The Sunset Garden of Memories." This cemetery was located across the street from the Historic Woodlawn Cemetery and was abandoned in the 1970s. After it fell into disrepair, the city disinterred all 117 people buried there and relocated them to the Palm Memorial Park on South Eastern Avenue. Palm Memorial Park, where all the burials were relocated to, is about one block from Sunset Park.

Much misinformation leads many to believe that Sunset Park was once a cemetery. This legend is hotly debated, even though there is no substantial evidence for the assertion.

32

THE GOLDEN TIKI

CHINATOWN

The Golden Tiki, a popular Polynesian nightspot in the heart of Chinatown, has an exciting history of paranormal activity. Many tourists who visit the Golden Tiki come for the fantastic vibe and stay to learn more about the spirits that stick around.

Staff at the Golden Tiki believe that the site was the location of a gruesome shooting dating back to 1995. This may cause the paranormal activity the employees experience. According to the stories, on January 14, 1995, four masked people entered the restaurant and started shooting people. Three people were shot. Much of the reported activity occurs in areas where shootings occurred.

Claims of paranormal activity at this restaurant include the apparition of a young girl, moving objects and flying shadow figures.[52] Poltergeist activity experienced at this location includes ashtrays moving across tables, strange EMF readings near objects and a glass shattering as it sat on a table.

The owner, Brandon Powers, created a unique collection of artifacts, the Museum of the Strange. Several paranormal researchers believe that his collection draws spirits to the tiki bar. Among the items on display at the Golden Tiki include black velvet paintings, a mummified mermaid, fertility idols and the skeleton of a mythical pirate, Captain William Tobias Faulkner.

Other peculiar objects found scattered throughout the restaurant include a sword and machetes rumored to be used to remove heads during rituals. In addition, a medicine bag that belonged to a shaman is housed at the restaurant and is one of the many objects that cause EMF detectors to spike.

If this collection of strange and possibly haunted objects wasn't creepy enough, the Golden Tiki is home to a vast collection of replicas of shrunken heads of famous entertainers, including Carrot Top, Robin Leach, magician Murray Sawchuck and Tape Face. (They are not authentic shrunken heads, but they are creepy and give off a spooky vibe.)

Something creepy is going on at the Golden Tiki, making it a fun place to visit and explore. Is it paranormal? There is a good chance that this location is haunted.

33

BINION'S GAMBLING HALL

nother location with many legends and ghost stories attached to its history is the Hotel Apache in Binion's Gambling Hall. Supernatural stories pass through the halls of this hotel from employee to employee, and many guests and visitors have picked up on a few of them, taking the accounts home and sharing them with friends and family.

One of the most commonly shared stories about this part of Sin City is set in Room 279 of the Hotel Apache, which opened in 1932. The story claims that a housekeeper turned around to find footprints on the floor she had just finished mopping. She was alone in the room when this occurred. Another employee reported having their hair pulled while in the hotel.

Many employees and guests experience strange occurrences in the Hotel Apache, and paranormal researchers believe that the hotel is haunted by the spirits of mobster Benny Binion and his wife, Teddy Jane. Binion purchased the hotel in 1951, and it became the primary residence for his wife and two sons.

Benny and Teddy Jane are believed to haunt the rooms above the casino floor.[53] Other paranormal activities reported include employees and guests hearing voices and strange sounds, seeing shadows and witnessing objects move around. Sounds of moving furniture have been reported in rooms that have been sealed off or where it has been confirmed that no one else was present.[54]

Some strange occurrences are happening at Binion's Gambling Hall. But with connections to the mob and nefarious activity conducted within the walls of the Hotel Apache, it is surprising that so little actual paranormal activity occurs here.

34

Red Rock Canyon National Conservation Area

Red Rock Canyon National Conservation Area has been visited and explored for more than ten thousand years, dating to when the Paleo-Archaic people lived there. Since then, many have come and gone, including pioneers, prospectors and tourists who leave the land with exciting and unique stories.

This beautiful site is located about fifteen miles west of Las Vegas and features bright-red limestone and sandstone formations, some reaching as high as 1,800 feet. Several rock formations can be seen from anywhere in the Vegas Valley.

Though Red Rock Canyon is beautiful and fun to explore, several mysterious occurrences have left many people questioning if the hills are haunted. Several hikers have reported seeing an ominous glow and pulsating lights in the hills while hiking at night. One hiker claimed that she was followed to her car by two balls of light that looked like eyes floating high off the ground. She claimed that the lights were too high to be those of an animal. They stayed some distance back from her but followed until she reached her vehicle.

Other people who have visited the conservation area have reported feeling being watched and creepy sensations in certain areas, especially near the petroglyphs on the rocks within the canyon. Others have reported seeing strange lights in the sky, several of which are believed to be from UFOs, a common occurrence in southern Nevada.

Left: Entrance stone at Red Rock Canyon's visitors center. *Heather Leigh.*

Below: Eerie clouds hang over Red Rock Canyon hiking trails. *Heather Leigh.*

Parts of Red Rock Canyon are desolate, with little vegetation. *Heather Leigh*.

Willow Spring trail entrance at Red Rock Canyon. *Heather Leigh*.

Red Rock Canyon is the subject of several urban legends, including the story that there is something sinister and extremely negative in the hills. This legend is tied to the fact that many people have mysteriously disappeared and died from accidents related to rock climbing.

The canyon has also been the site of many suicides, leading people to believe that something negative is attached to the canyon.

With such a long history of inhabitants and visitors, anything could lurk in Red Rock Canyon's hills.

35

BLUE DIAMOND, NEVADA

Not far from Red Rock Canyon and away from the bright lights of the Strip was a haunted site. It was a popular tourist attraction for travelers looking for a Wild West experience. Until it closed and was sold, Bonnie Springs Ranch in Blue Diamond, Nevada, offered a place for the living to experience life in the Old West and for spirits a place to call home.

Before westward expansion, this area was home to the Paiute people. Then travelers started making their way west to California on the Old Spanish Trail. Built in 1843 as a stopover for wagon trains headed to California, Bonnie Springs Ranch did not become a popular attraction until 1958. That is when Bonnie McGaugh and Al Levinson brought the ranch back to life, opening it as a tourist attraction complete with stables, a petting zoo, museums and a restaurant.

They created a new world, where employees portrayed life in the 1880s, when the area was a mining community. Many of the buildings were original and were restored to their former glory. With such an assortment of historic structures and reenactors walking the streets of the ranch, there is no wonder that spirits decided to stick around.

Several reports and claims by employees, visitors and paranormal researchers involved spirits roaming the property. For example, the spirit of a schoolgirl was spotted frolicking on the grounds in the afterlife, and a fussy older man sought privacy and did everything possible to avoid the living.

The schoolhouse was haunted by a former schoolteacher and the spirit of the schoolgirl. The girl also caused the merry-go-round on the property to spin. Some people who were lucky enough to see the ghost girl playing in the schoolhouse said that she immediately disappeared whenever someone noticed her.

The wax museum at the ranch was a popular attraction, showcasing various figures in period attire. It was one of the most-talked-about haunted locations on the property. If the tunnel-like maze was not creepy enough, there are claims that the wax figures came alive in the winding corridors. Witnesses claimed to have seen the figures move, to have been touched by them as they walked by and even to have noticed that spirits appeared to be breathing.

At one point in the history of the wax museum, workers nailed the wax figures to the floor to keep them in place. But this strategy did not work, and there were reports that the statues still moved.

Another sinister place at Bonnie Springs Ranch was the opera house, where it was believed that an evil entity existed. It would form a dark shadow figure that followed people throughout the building. This shadowy figure was captured in photographs. The opera house was where many disturbing EVPs were captured.

Unfortunately, Bonnie Springs Ranch was permanently closed and sold in 2019, leaving the spirits behind, wondering where they will haunt next.

36

MORE LAS VEGAS GHOST STORIES

5285 DEAN MARTIN DRIVE

This site is visible from I-15. Over the years, many residents and visitors have noticed that this building tends to be tenant-free more often than it houses a business. Everything from Epic to Hidden Secrets to a Mexican restaurant to a soul food joint have come and gone, with no company sticking around for too long.

If 5285 Dean Martin Drive was not haunted, it sure was cursed. Paranormal investigators who have studied the building claim that something otherworldly was going on within the structure.

One urban legend claims that the mob once used this area as a place to bury bodies. Research, however, has not been able to confirm this legend. But that happens with most legends associated with Las Vegas mob activity. Lots of legends but very little proof.

After several fires caused by some of the homeless who frequent the area, the building was torn down. The site is now used for overflow parking for Raiders games at Allegiant Stadium.[55]

Was the building at 5285 Dean Martin Drive along West Hacienda Avenue haunted? Unfortunately, because it was demolished, we may never know the answer.

6660 Pecos

If the address doesn't say it all, then the evil spirits lurking in the shadows at the home at 6660 Pecos in Las Vegas will convince you this location is haunted. The home, located across the street from the entrance to Wayne Newton's Casa de Shenandoah estate, has had trouble holding on to owners. The house has had a revolving door of owners, as it appears the home keeps going back up for sale.

Could owners' lack of desire to keep this property have anything to do with the ghost of a teenage girl rumored to have been tortured in satanic rituals performed by members of the Hells Angels before being killed? When it comes to the paranormal, anything is possible.

According to the legend, the girl was kidnapped by men believed to be Hells Angels. There is no proof it was them, so they may have been members of another biker gang. The girl's body was discovered long after the bikers had left the premises, as were several satanic blood marks on the walls and floors.

Though no one knows why this home cannot seem to hold on to its owners, if the spirit of the girl or of any former members of the biker gang or negative satanic energy still lingers on the property, that could be a good indication of the problem.

The Cromwell

The Cromwell opened in the 1970s and is one of the oldest hotels in the area. In 2020, the hotel was transformed into an adults-only property to fit its "garden of earthly delights" theme.

Like several other properties in Las Vegas, the Cromwell has a dark past, including a rash of mysterious deaths. These deaths have left a psychic imprint on the property. Several guests report feeling watched and hearing intrusive voices impeding their thoughts, commanding them to do drastic and heinous activities.

Could these voices be the spirits of the past continuing to cause mayhem in the afterlife? Or are these voices encouraging many to be violent and vicious, creating the dark history of the Cromwell?

There is no definitive answer, as not much else is known about the Cromwell and its paranormal activity.

HARTLAND MANSION

What mansion is not spooky? The Lemp Mansion in St. Louis, Missouri? There are some eerie legends attached to this home. The Haunted Mansion at Walt Disney World? Creepy. The Hartland Mansion? Some stories shed a spooky shimmer over this Sin City mansion.

The Hartland Mansion is one place in Vegas that cannot be skipped in discussions of legends, lore and ghost stories. This luxurious mansion was the setting for swanky wedding receptions and high school formals and was even featured in movies, including *Casino*.

This downtown Vegas home was haunted by more than just the spirit of a cranky mobster. It is believed to be a popular place for the spirit of Elvis to escape to when he is not haunting the Westgate Las Vegas Hotel and Casino.

Young Elvis is believed to have spent the night here, and his is one spirit making appearances in this landmark, partying in spirit with celebrities who hosted events at the mansion, including Frank Sinatra, Ginger Rogers and Michael Jackson. In addition, CeeLo Green, the Muppets and Gene Simmons of KISS filmed videos at the Hartland Mansion. Chances are that there is a lot of built-up energy helping to fuel paranormal activity in the home.

When it comes to paranormal activity in the Hartland Mansion, there is a possibility that it results from overflow hauntings at Zak Bagans' The Haunted Museum, which is across the street.[56]

More recently, the Hartland Mansion has been the site for Las Vegas Fire and Rescue to perform training drills. The last report about the thirty-one-thousand-square-foot Hartland Mansion stated that it was up for demolition within the week after the training was completed.

JW MARRIOTT LAS VEGAS RESORT & SPA

The JW Marriott Las Vegas Resort & Spa is located northwest of the central Strip area and is a popular place for business travelers to stay. Few claims of paranormal activity have been reported at this resort, but according to one story, what happened is very interesting.

A businessman staying at the JW Marriott in the Summerlin resort area was woken up in the middle of the night to a bright white glow from the bathroom. The swing arm mirror light was turned on, but it had not been on before the man went to bed. He turned it off and returned to his slumber.

When he and his friend decided to leave, he left the room exclaiming, "It's all yours." He claims to have heard a whistle similar to the sound "whhhhooooooo" and felt a soft slap on his left ear.

He shared his story with his friend, who said it might have been the air-conditioning. But after experiencing it firsthand, the businessman doubted that was the explanation. Finally, his friend shared the story with the valet, who asked, "What floor?" They told him it was the fifth floor, and the valet responded, "I have heard of stuff on the sixth floor, but not much on the fifth floor."

Shocked by the answer, the two left. No other information about this story is available.

THE PALOMINO CLUB

The Palomino Club's owner, Adam Gentile, is no stranger to paranormal activity. His club, located across from Jerry's Nugget in North Las Vegas, is considered a hot spot for strange occurrences and paranormal incidents. This fully nude strip club was founded in 1969. In 2000, it was the site of the high-profile murder of an employee at the hands of the owner's son, Jack Perry.

Gentile took ownership of the club in 2006 after his father, Domenick Gentile, was granted ownership in exchange for representing the Palomino Club's former owner, Luis Hidalgo Jr., who was facing charges for the shooting death of Timothy Hadland. Hadland was a former doorman for the club. His body was found near Lake Mead, where many more bodies appeared in 2022 after the waters receded due to drought.

Undoubtedly, the Palomino Club is home to dark and negative energies that have been affecting the staff.

Legend claims that there was a dancer who committed suicide in the club. No one today remembers her. It is rumored that the spirit of this dancer came through to a psychic, asking for help to move on. There is not much other information about this incident or if the spirit is still hanging around. But it makes for an eerie legend that could be the source of some of the crazy paranormal activity at the club.

Employees have spotted dark figures darting around the club, the sounds of disembodied voices and multiple EVPs. For example, Zak Bagans and the crew of *Ghost Adventures* investigated the club for an episode of the Travel Channel show. Zak asked, "Are you still here?" He received a female EVP response: "I'm still here."

Several local paranormal teams have investigated the Palomino Club and reported that they believe the club is haunted. Reports of paranormal activity include disembodied voices, light anomalies, shadow figures, full-bodied apparitions and strange, uneasy feelings when wandering the club in the dark.

37
LAS VEGAS URBAN LEGENDS

L as Vegas is home to many myths and urban legends, so the city is often considered a dangerous place to visit. Of course, there is no proof that these legends are true, but they are something to think about. Here are some of the most common urban legends in Sin City.

THE MEGABUCKS CURSE

The Megabucks Curse has made its way to this hotel. It started with rumors about a cocktail waitress at the Desert Inn who won the Megabucks jackpot worth $34.9 million at the hotel. Unfortunately, immediately after winning, she was involved in an auto accident and was wheelchair-bound for the remainder of her life.

This curse is rumored to have taken the lives of several people who won at the Megabucks slot machine in Vegas. Rumored deaths include victims of a fatal overdose, a plane crash, a gang fight and a heart attack.

THE CORPSE UNDER THE BED

This classic story is similar to the one featured in the 1995 film *Four Rooms* starring Tim Roth, Quentin Tarantino, Antonio Banderas and Salma Hayek.

As the story goes, a couple checks into their Las Vegas hotel room and immediately calls down to the front desk to complain about the room having a foul odor. Unfortunately, the hotel is fully booked, so the couple cannot change rooms. But the hotel staff come up to try cleaning the room again. The additional cleaning does not work, and the stench continues to linger.

The couple goes out for the night to gamble and returns to go to bed. They try to sleep, but the smell is so unbearable that they begin to search their room for the source. Finally, they lift the mattress and discover a rotting corpse underneath it.

A variation of this story involves the couple sleeping through the night and calling the front desk first thing in the morning to help identify the source of the odor. On investigation, the body of a dead prostitute is discovered under the bed they were sleeping on.

Could this be a true story? It's possible, especially if it occurred when the mob ruled the Strip. However, this story is a common one, and many major cities have similar versions.

THE KIDNEY BLACK MARKET

Another classic urban legend in Las Vegas involves a lonely tourist who goes to a bar and encounters locals. The new friends share some drinks, but the tourist's beverage is spiked. Waking up, he finds himself in an ice-filled bathtub with stitches. Next to the tub, he finds a note telling him to call 911 if he wants to live. His kidney has been removed to be sold on the black market.

In another version of this story, an unsuspecting business traveler meets an attractive young woman in a bar, and the two hit it off. She invites him to her hotel room, where they enjoy more drinks. The man is then drugged. After he passes out, gang members surgically remove his kidney and leave him in a bathtub of ice. This story also features a note next to the tub: "Call 911 if you want to live."

This story was shared on the internet, and many businesspeople have forwarded it to colleagues who might be traveling to Vegas.

Though an urban legend, the story became so widespread that the National Kidney Foundation has asked anyone who has had their kidney illegally removed to come forward and share their story. So far, no one has come forward.

DIGGING UP AND REBURYING MAFIA BODIES

When construction in Summerlin, located thirty minutes from the Las Vegas Strip, began, construction workers kept digging up bodies believed to be buried in the area by the mafia. When the bodies were discovered, construction halted to allow a forensic investigator to check out the site.

Because that incident delayed construction, rumor has it, workers were instructed to cover up any bodies they discovered and pretend they were not there. There is no proof that this occurred, but if it did, the owners of the million-dollar homes in Summerlin might be in for interesting paranormal activity—if they are not experiencing it already.

MYSTERIOUS RADIO CALL SIGN "JANET"

McCarran Airport is about six hundred miles northwest of Roswell and fewer than ninety miles from the infamous Area 51. There were reports of a mysterious plane taking off and landing at McCarran Airport, now known as Harry Reid International Airport, using the radio call sign "Janet." No schedule or manifest was filed for this plane. Adding to the

Aerial view of Las Vegas, Nevada, looking toward the airport and down on the turreted towers of the Excalibur Hotel and Casino (*lower right*). *Library of Congress.*

mystery is the fact that no one knew the aircraft's destination or where it was coming from.

The mystery surrounding this plane has fueled many conspiracy theories and legends. Many believe that these flights carried military scientists to and from a secret U.S. Air Force base nearby. UFO enthusiasts believe the planes were headed to Area 51, a secure military base south of Rachel, Nevada.[57]

Anything is possible. After all, Area 51 is a popular place for people to try to get into, but with its high level of security, it is challenging to get a glimpse of the base. Nevertheless, several people have reported strange occurrences and UFO activity along the Extraterrestrial Highway, Nevada State Route 375.

PART II
HENDERSON

38

CLARK COUNTY MUSEUM

Goldfield is about 185 miles north of the Vegas Valley and is believed to be the most haunted living ghost town in the Silver State. But did you know that a piece of Goldfield history is set in Henderson, Nevada? The Clark County Heritage Museum has many restored buildings on display as part of Heritage Street, where the Giles-Barcus House now stands.

The Giles-Barcus House was originally in Goldfield before it was moved in 1955 by Edith Giles Barcus, daughter of the home's owner, Edwin Schofield Giles, to Las Vegas. She did not want to leave her childhood home behind and moved the building to downtown Las Vegas, where it was an antiques shop for many years. She donated the house at her death to the Clark County Heritage Museum, where it has been ever since.[58]

The eerie feeling in the building is hard to describe, as it is both welcoming and has a touch of "get out of my home." Some visitors have claimed to see the apparition of an older woman wearing a velvet dress in the corner of the home, but she does not interact with anyone. She continues with what she is doing before she fades away. Because this spirit does not seem to interact with anyone or notice that anyone is around, it is believed to be the product of residual energy left behind by the former owner's wife, Edith Corlis Giles, or his daughter.

The Beckley House, originally on Fourth Street in downtown Las Vegas, is rumored to have the spirit of a young girl roaming the home. The museum's former curator, Mark Hall-Patton, the "Beard of Knowledge" on the

The Giles-Barcus House at the Clark County Museum in Henderson, Nevada. *Heather Leigh.*

History Channel's *Pawn Stars* and Motion Picture Video's *Real Haunts: Ghost Towns* and *Real Haunts 3*, stated that no child has died in that home or in any neighboring residence. The idea that someone has to die in a house for it to be haunted is a myth, so the spirit, if there is one in this building, could be that of a child attached to the land, or one who decided to stay in the home because she liked it.[59]

Some visitors have claimed to see an older man at the Berkeley House and a prankster spirit that likes to disturb the bedsheets and leave depressions on the bedspread. In addition, some people have heard unexplained moans from within the empty house. Maintenance workers cannot find the source of the sounds.

The former residence of Las Vegas businessman Prosper J. Goumand now stands on Heritage Street at the Clark County Heritage Museum, where there have been many reports of paranormal activity. Many who enter feel sad. A young, thin woman sometimes appears in the doorway of the home. If anyone approaches her, she disappears. A sizable, ghostly cat lingers around the home and disappears when someone reaches down to pet it or pick it up.

Antique vehicle sits along the back trails at the Clark County Museum. *Heather Leigh*.

The Townsite House, built in 1942, was a temporary shelter for workers at a magnesium plant; it is now on Heritage Street and is home to a lot of energy. Many people feel sadness when they enter the child's room. Legends allude to this structure having unknown, dark secrets.

Cemetery display entrance at the Clark County Museum. *Heather Leigh.*

Wild West cemetery display at the Clark County Museum. *Heather Leigh.*

Grave displays at the Clark County Museum. *Heather Leigh.*

On the back side of the museum is an Old West town with a cemetery along the walking path. Several old buildings cater to a new Wild West setting, including a creepy barn. Walking up to the barn, the author and her son witnessed the door opening on its own. And when they entered the barn, the door closed behind them.

Did a spirit open the door for them? It is possible. But it is also possible that wind opened the door. Either way, it was creepy and coincidental that the door opened at the perfect time.

Is the Clark County Heritage Museum haunted? Many personal experiences, urban legends and stories are being shared, but there is no evidence that the museum is haunted. This museum is one place you must see for yourself and determine if it is haunted based on your personal experiences.

39

McCAW SCHOOL OF MINES

McCaw School of Mines, a hidden gem in the heart of Henderson, Nevada, is home to mining memorabilia and an aboveground simulated mine experience. The museum is adjacent to the Gordon McCaw STEAM Academy campus, where the idea of the mine experience started in a teacher's classroom. The efforts of Principal Janet Dobry in the early 1990s helped bring McCaw School of Mines to life. Executive Director Philip Luna helped keep this vision alive by educating children about the mining industry and its history.[60]

The mine experience, with a design similar to that of the Indiana Jones ride at Disneyland, is the only simulated underground in Nevada. The 5,100-square-foot underground mine replica was dedicated in 1996. The 3,000-square-foot visitors center was added to the museum in 2000.

Until the author and the paranormal team she was on offered to help with a Halloween event in 2019, there had been no reports of paranormal activity occurring at the museum. She and her team took groups on mine tours, showing them how paranormal investigations went. Guess what? They had a lot of interactions and collected a ton of evidence. It was almost as if the spirits were waiting for someone to recognize them and were excited to have someone to interact with.

During the Halloween tours, the team conducted EVP sessions with a spirit box in one of the mine rooms. During these sessions, they received intelligent responses, including answers to questions asked by the author's son.

Entrance to the simulated mine experience at McCaw School of Mines. *Heather Leigh*.

The visitors center at McCaw School of Mines in Henderson, Nevada. *Heather Leigh.*

Question: Is a tomato a fruit or a vegetable?
Answer: Fruit

Question: Is the earth flat or round?
Answer: Round

From the answers, it is obvious that the team communicated with an intelligent spirit that enjoyed interacting with the living. By asking questions outside the traditional paranormal ghost-hunting topics, the team got some fantastic responses.

A train was donated to the museum by Area 51, and strange occurrences have been noted near the train. The author and another paranormal researcher spotted the feet of a small child between the railcar and the tracks. Further investigation revealed no child on the other side of the train or anywhere in the vicinity.

EMF readings around this car were higher than at any other car on the faux railway. When using an ovilus, investigators believed they were communicating with a boy between the ages of nine and twelve.

The railcar from Area 51 is one of the most haunted items at McCaw School of Mines. *Heather Leigh.*

Behind the train, near the visitors center, is a cart that was used to bring miners up from the mine. During an EVP session, the author heard loud bangs from inside the coach. Another investigator brought a fidget spinner. They were able to communicate with a spirit in the area, which started slowly spinning the device.

A team used dowsing rods in the back of the mine, where there is an elevator cage from Nelson, Nevada. During the session, a spirit actively interacted with the team, answering yes-and-no questions as they opened and closed the rods.

In the same area where the elevator cage is located, the author experienced many feelings, including happiness and sadness. While volunteering during an event, a child approached her and wanted her to thank the man dressed in overalls and a hard hat for taking the time to talk to him. Knowing that none of the volunteers was dressed like that, the author went to see who was there. The area was empty. She believes that the child had seen and interacted with the apparition of the miner, who she has only caught glimpses of as a darting shadow figure in the area near the elevator cage.

Above: View from the mine shaft elevator at McCaw School of Mines. *Heather Leigh*.

Opposite: Miners on display at McCaw School of Mines. *Heather Leigh*.

The second room in the mine is one of the most active areas, and the author has had several interactions there with a spirit. Douglas Dresner, whose personal belongings are on display, hangs around the mine, watching over his items. Whenever the author entered and left this room, she would say "hello" and "goodbye." Nine times out of ten, she heard a response from a disembodied voice.

The author's husband had an experience in the same room. He went into the room to cool off and, when leaving, said, "Thank you for letting me come in and cool off." He heard, "You're welcome" as he walked out. He was the only one in the mine at the time.

The author conducted an EVP session one day in the room. She was alone. During the session, she asked if the spirit could swing the birdcage hanging in the room. Nothing happened. She asked if it could move the poles leaning against the wall. Still nothing. Something caught her eye on the shelf on the other side of the room. She bent down to look at the item, and when she stood up, she hit her head on the birdcage. She heard a disembodied laugh the moment she hit her head.

In other incident, a black mass came out of nowhere and rushed up to the author, who was taking a video of the room. Further review revealed that

Above: Looking up from inside the simulated mine experience at McCaw School of Mines. *Heather Leigh*.

Opposite, top: Douglas Dresner's personal belongings, donated by his wife, are on display at McCaw School of Mines. *Heather Leigh*.

Opposite, bottom: Image of a tommy-knocker caught on film in a Nevada mine. *Heather Leigh*.

Mines, Mining Camps & A Tommy-Knocker

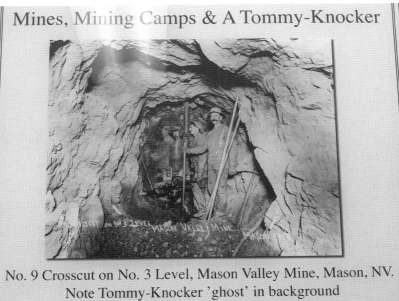

No. 9 Crosscut on No. 3 Level, Mason Valley Mine, Mason, NV.
Note Tommy-Knocker 'ghost' in background
Nevada Historical Society

Campsite display at McCaw School of Mines, where the sign is often disturbed overnight. *Heather Leigh.*

there was nothing on the video. She is still unsure what happened, because that has never happened since.

The mine has a display in the visitors center with an image of a tommy-knocker. These creative and witty creatures were common in mines and often blamed for devastating events. It is believed that when you hear the knocks of the tommy-knocker, it was time to get out of the mine. In many situations, when the miners heard the knock of the tommy-knocker and they evacuated the mine, the shaft would collapse moments later. Were the knocks of these mischievous creatures a warning, or did the sound emanate from the mine walls cracking before collapsing? Anything is possible, especially with all of the legends and supernatural occurrences in the mines throughout Nevada.

Nothing dangerous is hanging around McCaw School of Mines in the afterlife. It is a lot of residual energy; harmless spirits hang around where they are comfortable.

40
THREE KIDS MINE

Three Kids Mine, also known as the Wheel of Misfortune, is a roadside attraction off the beaten path in Henderson, Nevada. This site is twenty miles southeast of the Las Vegas Strip and is a one-of-a-kind location in southern Nevada.

Three Kids Mine was a manganese mine that operated from 1917 to 1961. Since operations ceased, the location has become a popular graffiti

Three Kids Mine, aka the "Wheel of Misfortune," is located near Lake Las Vegas in Henderson, Nevada. *Heather Leigh*.

site. Many visitors explore the site by standing on the edge of the massive, wheel-like structures.

Three Kids Mine became known as the Wheel of Misfortune in 2012 after artist Aware painted a "Wheel of Fortune" on the structures. Since the property has been reimagined, graffiti artists have left their marks on the remaining structures of the mine.

Located near Lake Las Vegas along trail mile markers 9.0 to 10.5, Three Kids Mine is a significant part of southern Nevada's mining history. The site was inactive for many years, until it was used for two movies. Although there were plans to clean up the area, it remains in disrepair, and many homeless persons reside in the shafts of the mine.

Because Three Kids Mine is not a common place for people to visit ("No trespassing" signs have recently been posted), there are not many stories of paranormal activity at the location.

Visitors have claimed to see shadow people and to hear strange noises and howling in the mine shafts. Unfortunately, because the site is not secure, it is nearly impossible to determine if the reports are related to the paranormal or if people living in the tunnels are making the noises.

41
FOX RIDGE PARK

According to paranormal researchers, Fox Ridge Park is one of the most haunted parks in the Vegas Valley area. But many researchers debate whether this property is haunted or if the stories are the stuff of urban legend.

The most commonly told story is of a young boy killed near the park. Unfortunately, he remains behind to haunt those who dare to enter the park at night.

During the day, Fox Ridge Park is a popular destination for families and outdoor enthusiasts. The park features play areas, barbecue grills, sports courts and large fields. Visiting this park during the day, it is hard to believe that there is any paranormal activity attached to it. But when the sun sets, it is thought that the park is not only haunted by the spirit of a young boy but also that this boy is demonic and turns evil the moment anyone approaches him.

According to the legend, the boy was killed by a drunk driver near the park. Several claim that the swings will move on their own, thought to be the boy playing in the afterlife. This spirit does not like to be looked at. It is rumored that if someone looks him in the eyes, the spirit turns into a demonic vision and quickly vanishes.

In addition to seeing the swings move, several people have claimed to see the spirit of a young boy walking around the park and disappearing when they approach him. Other paranormal stories reported at Fox Ridge Park include seeing shadow figures and mists moving around the playground and feeling a sense of unease, almost as if someone is watching you while at the park at night.

Paranormal investigators have concocted several studies at this park and claim to have captured EVPs of a boy's voice. Researchers have experienced equipment malfunctions and seeing shadow figures in the distance wandering the park.

Several paranormal investigators discount the presence of ghosts at Fox Ridge Park, leading many to believe the stories are urban legends passed along for entertainment purposes. Whether or not the park is haunted, the stories make for entertaining information to keep in mind when visiting this quiet park at night.

42

GREEN VALLEY PARK

Green Valley Park in Henderson is a popular gathering place for families looking for wide-open, green spaces to run around and play. It is one of the most popular parks in the town south of the Las Vegas Strip and allows families to feel like they are not living so close to Sin City.

According to legend, two boys were killed in the 1970s and their bodies dumped in the park. Because court records are sealed, those who share this story have trouble verifying the claim. Nevertheless, several spirits have been seen near the barbecue area and the front area of the park, and it is believed that these ghosts are of the two boys who were left at the park.

Another urban legend attached to Green Valley Park involves another person whose body was found there. The family of the man found in the park placed a plaque and buried a tree with the name *Christopher Brown* engraved in the plaque. There was a Henderson resident by the name of Christopher D. Brown. He died while attempting to cross Interstate 15 on foot, so the memorial plaque may be for him.

But what is the origin of the legend of his body being dumped and found in the park? It is interesting how myths develop, and they can sometimes lead astray researchers and those who are curious about paranormal activity.

The author had an opportunity to learn about paranormal activity from Brian J. Rollins, cofounder of SisBro Paranormal, and Gary Colley. Both are paranormal investigators, and they shared the story about Christopher Brown with the author about their experiences at Green Valley Park.

RUSSIAN ROULETTE?

The following story includes facts from a *Las Vegas Sun* article of June 13, 2018,[61] and a *Las Vegas Review-Journal* report of December 10, 2019.[62]

On Friday, June 8, 2018, in the afternoon, a group of teens met at an abandoned house in the 2000 block of Cool Lilac Lane. It was supposed to be a gathering to play Russian roulette. In actuality, it was a setup for a "friend."

Before playing the game, one teen, Jaiden Caruso, filmed himself with a Ruger .357 revolver. The weapon was loaded with one bullet. Kody Harlan witnessed the events, and Jaiden was the only person in the house to touch the gun. He later bragged about how he had "caught a body." He also panned the camera to capture different angles of the mortally wounded "friend," Matthew Minkler, who died during the incident.

The two teens and others left the house soon after. Before leaving, Kody took the wallet from Matthew. No one attempted to render any aid.

After initially leaving the area, Caruso and Harlan returned to the scene. They covered the boy in plastic, dragged his body to a closet and left it inside. The door of the closet was spray-painted with an expletive. The inscription reportedly was directed at the victim.

The northeast corner of Green Valley Park in Henderson, Nevada. *Brian J. Rollins.*

Railroad tracks at Green Valley Park. *Brian J. Rollins.*

Hours later, a group of paranormal investigators, including myself and Gary Colley, were doing a training session at Green Valley Park. While investigating one corner of the park, I looked out toward the railroad tracks. I noticed three males walking.

I pointed this out to Gary as they turned and started walking in our direction. They came over and hopped a wall. We moved our group over so that they could pass. By this time, only two males had gone by. We never saw the third male. He had disappeared.

The paranormal training was stopped, and I told everyone what we had just witnessed. We quickly went over to the tracks and looked for the other juvenile. We saw no one in either direction. Nor did anyone see this third male hop the wall into the housing on the other side of the tracks.

We broke out some equipment and started an investigation. We used several devices that read electric and magnetic fields (EMF). Several EVPs were captured, and the paranormal investigation team may have recorded evidence of the third male as an apparition. No other devices caught anything.

Later in the evening, Jaiden and Kody stole a Mercedes and got into a crash. This occurred after Henderson police attempted to stop them. During an inspection of the vehicle, a gun was found. The weapon was a .357 Ruger with a spent cartridge still in it.

Railroad tracks at Green Valley Park. *Brian J. Rollins.*

Entrance to Green Valley Park in Henderson, Nevada. *Brian J. Rollins.*

Railroad tracks at Green Valley Park. *Brian J. Rollins.*

Green Valley Park sign. *Brian J. Rollins.*

In August 2019, both suspects were sentenced to life in prison with the possibility of parole. They had been found guilty of first-degree murder and robbery with a deadly weapon. Kody Harden was also convicted of accessory to murder. Both have the possibility of getting out in 2039.

Was the third juvenile male Matthew Minkler? Could it have been someone else who we couldn't find? How could someone appear so soon after death? Will we ever get the answers? Further investigation, by myself and others, will have to be done to answer these questions.

PART III

BOULDER CITY

43

BOULDER DAM HOTEL

For years, paranormal stories have involved strange occurrences at the Boulder Dam Hotel in Boulder City. Visitors and employees share experiences of hearing chilling noises in empty halls and sounds of music from empty rooms.

The hotel was built during the Hoover Dam's construction and has been the place for foreign dignitaries, celebrities and politicians to stay in southern Nevada. For example, Howard Hughes spent time at the hotel while recovering from injuries he suffered during his 1943 plane crash into Lake Mead.

Henry Smith designed the hotel, which was influenced by the colonial revival style and is now listed in the National Register of Historic Places.

An employee once heard laughing, talking and music coming from the closed ballroom and restaurant. The employee also reported smelling cigar smoke from these rooms when no one was there.

Sounds of running water are heard in the restrooms. After an investigation of the sounds, the bathroom door quickly slammed shut behind the employee. The same employee reported seeing the elevator doors open for no reason in the basement.

Other reports of paranormal activity at the Boulder Dam Hotel include the feeling of heaviness and a sense of being unwelcome in the lobby. Some guests have reported feeling like hands were reaching up from the floor and grabbing their ankles.

Rooms 209 and 219 are the most haunted locations in the hotel, often causing guests to change rooms or check out early.

The most famous ghost at the hotel is that of former night clerk Tommy Thompson. The apparition of Thompson is seen walking the halls and getting into the elevator, where he disappears before reaching the next floor.

There is no doubt that the Boulder Dam Hotel is one of the most haunted locations in Boulder City.

44

RAILROAD TUNNELS

The Railroad Tunnels in Boulder City are a unique location. Explorers can walk through multiple tunnels. Built in the 1930s, these tunnels were used to transport goods and supplies to the Hoover Dam during its construction.

After running all day and every day, the tracks were dismantled in 1961 and 1962. Today, the trails through the tunnels take hikers on a journey with breathtaking views of the Boulder Basin.

People walking through these tunnels experience an eerie feeling. Some people have claimed to hear strange sounds and disembodied voices. It is common to walk through the tunnels hearing footsteps close behind.

Historic American Engineering Record, Creator, Engineer U.S. Bureau Of Reclamation, and Inc. Six Companies. Hoover Dam, Nevada Spoils Tunnel, near the Lower Portal Tunnel Access Road, Boulder City, Clark County, Nevada. *Library of Congress*.

With the Railroad Tunnel Trail extending 8.2 miles, the tunnels may create an echo-chamber effect, bringing sounds from one end of a tunnel to the other. When this happens, the noises, footsteps and voices people hear could be coming from someone they cannot see farther down the trail.

Though there may be natural explanations for the strange sounds, many men died during the construction of the Hoover Dam, so it is possible that the tunnels are home to spirits hanging around their former work location.

45

THE BOULDER CITY PET CEMETERY

In the middle of the desert near Boulder City is a plot of land with a mysterious past. The Boulder City Pet Cemetery was an unauthorized venue that was home to many rumors and speculation about what was buried there.

The exact date this plot of land started to be used as a pet cemetery is unknown. Many people speculate that veterinarian Marwood Doud created it in the 1950s. Others believe the cemetery illegally began in the 1930s. Finally, some rumors claim that Emory Lockette, a civil engineer, developed the cemetery in 1953 and offered pet funeral services for fifty dollars.

The cemetery is the final resting place for dogs, cats, other pets and possibly some humans. Local legend claims the that mafia secretly buried victims there, knowing that no one would look there for fear of disturbing the pets.

Boulder City purchased the land from the federal government in 1995 and dedicated the area as a Desert Tortoise Habitat. It has been illegal to bury pets at this cemetery since then. But gravestones have been spotted with dates as recent as 2015.

Walking through the pet cemetery, visitors see various types of graves, including rough, primitive graves and elaborate ones. The most famous resident at the pet cemetery is Flash, the son of film star Rin Tin Tin.

It is believed that this is the most haunted pet cemetery in the world, with reports of shadow figures, full-bodied apparitions and an overwhelming sense of doom. The most popular apparition is a white cat that has been

Several pets have been buried at the Boulder City Pet Cemetery. *Ryan MacMichael.*

known to rub against visitors' legs and disappear when picked up. The cat will follow visitors, but only if she likes them. Sounds of a small cat bell are heard ringing through the cemetery.

One disturbing legend is of a doglike creature, a combination of a dog and a mob victim, that appeared after their bones were washed together in a flood. This ghoulish mongrel roams the desert near the cemetery, searching for the mob boss who dumped his body there. Legend claims that this creature wants revenge and will not stop looking for its killer.

The pets buried at the Boulder City Pet Cemetery were well-loved, and their owners cared for them when creating their final resting place.

46
HOOVER DAM

Originally known as Boulder Dam, Hoover Dam was built in 1935, creating Lake Mead. The dam provided cities throughout Nevada, Southern California and Arizona with significant hydroelectric power and irrigation water.

Though many benefited from the dam's creation, several construction workers perished during its construction. At least 112 people died during the dam's construction, but it is believed that dozens more died from illnesses related to carbon monoxide poisoning from inside the structure.

The most widely spread legend about Hoover Dam has bodies trapped inside the dam's concrete. Stories claim that construction workers fell into the concrete as it was poured into place. This legend is unproven for several reasons, including the fact that the dam was made up of individual blocks poured elsewhere and then set in place. Second, if bodies were left in the concrete, over time they would have decomposed, leaving air pockets in the walls and the structure unstable.

Whether souls are believed to be trapped in the dam's walls or are the spirits of workers who died during construction, the dam is extremely haunted. Visitors and workers at the dam notice drastic temperature changes, both hot and cold, and many have heard sounds of water dripping when everything is operating as usual.

Apparitions walking through the tunnels surprise workers who do not expect to see anyone there. Spirits of the Hoover Dam are blamed for missing tools, similar to the effect of tommy-knockers in the mines.

Above: Statue of a Hoover Dam worker. *Heather Leigh*.

Opposite: Hoover Dam plaque in Boulder City, Nevada. *Heather Leigh*.

The Hoover Dam has been the site of more than one hundred suicides since 1935. In addition, the Mike O'Callaghan–Pat Tillman Memorial Bridge is the site of suicides and is now one of the most haunted bridges in Nevada.

In one interesting story, a cab driver driving over the bridge saw a woman crossing it. He said the woman looked distraught. He pulled over and got out to help the woman, but before he could get to her, she jumped over the bridge.

When he ran to the edge, he did not see her falling. It was as if she had disappeared. Several people have claimed to see the same apparition, only to have it disappear when it gets to the edge or jumps over it. It is not known if this is a spirit reliving someone's final moments before her death or if the vision is residual energy imprinted on the environment.

One sad story is that of a dog loved by all the workers on the dam and considered a part of the crew. It was known that if anyone messed with the dog, they would have to talk to the foreman about their behavior. The dog was agile and could quickly walk across platforms. He had a lunch box and ate with the men. He also lined up to get on the bus at the end of the workday.

This page, top: View of the Hoover Dam from the visitors center. *Heather Leigh.*

This page, bottom: View of the Mike O'Callaghan–Pat Tillman Memorial Bridge from the Hoover Dam. *Heather Leigh.*

Opposite: View of water heading out to Lake Mead from the Hoover Dam. *Heather Leigh.*

One day, the dog was fatally run over while sleeping under a truck. He was buried at the dam and has a memorial plaque. Since the dog's death, people have spotted shadows about the size and shape of a dog quickly maneuvering through the tunnels and restricted areas.

Undoubtedly, Hoover Dam is one of the most haunted locations in southern Nevada. It may be one of the most haunted locations in the country.

47

OLD BOULDER CITY HOSPITAL

The Old Boulder City Hospital was built during the Great Depression to accommodate and provide care for injured and ill construction workers. Often called the "Hospital of the Damned," this building was the final place where many Hoover Dam construction workers stayed before their death.

Hoover Dam deaths resulted from falls, being struck, cuts and what many claimed to have been pneumonia. Those who died from pneumonia were believed to have suffered carbon monoxide poisoning from working inside the dam. Many reports claim that the spirits of the men who died from pneumonia want answers for the coverup related to their deaths.

In 2012, the building became a community center, and residents knew they were not alone in the building. Visitors and employees reported hearing disembodied moans, voices and footsteps. Shadow figures and apparitions were spotted in the building.

The structure sat abandoned for many years, boarded up, preventing paranormal investigators from getting in to determine what haunted the building. The building is gone, but the spirits who haunted it have not been forgotten.

48

UFO SIGHTINGS

With Area 51 just a couple of hours away, the Las Vegas Valley area is a hot spot for UFO sightings. Most of the sightings are in Boulder City and nearby Searchlight, but it is possible to capture a glimpse of something from out of this world near the Las Vegas Strip.

When looking for UFOs in the area, be aware of other explanations for the strange lights in the sky. For example, many visitors confuse the lights from airplanes landing at Harry Reid International Airport. The skies over the Vegas Valley are so busy with air traffic, and it can be challenging to determine what is an alien craft and what is a plane full of tourists coming in for a landing.

One UFO sighting was reported by someone traveling from Los Angeles to Las Vegas. They were on the main road going into the city between Boulder City and Las Vegas. The area was very desolate, and not a lot of city lighting interfered with looking up at the stars.

While driving, the observer reported suddenly seeing six lights overhead. There was no sound. The lights were very bright and in a *V* shape. The person compared the image to military helicopters flying in formation. The lights were hovering about twenty to thirty feet above the ground and moving toward Las Vegas. The driver turned off the highway and stopped at a stop sign to observe the lights, which continued moving toward the city.

Could this incident be similar to what has been experienced by people who saw Phoenix Lights? Or could it be a military plane, similar to the Big Black Deltas?[63] Big Black Deltas are the large, black, triangular-shaped aircraft that are believed to be extraterrestrial. Without being there, and having no photographic evidence, the truth of this incident cannot be determined. But it makes for an exciting story.

Several eyewitnesses have reported UFO sightings in Boulder City to MUFON (the Mutual UFO Network). Some events date to 1980 but were not reported until 2014. The first local UFO sighting took place in Boulder City on Friday, April 4, 1980 (reported on August 27, 2014), involving two spheres hovering about three feet above a building. The observer claimed to be about fifteen feet from the spheres and did not feel afraid. The spheres did not have a light source but appeared lighter than the sky and had a defined outline.

There was no sound as the spheres moved, with the first slowly moving upward, followed by the second. Then they suddenly zipped toward the east before disappearing behind some trees.

Another interesting UFO experience was from a photographer in Henderson, who was shooting photos of an electrical storm on Wednesday, September 6, 2017, at Cornerstone Park. The observer was looking south toward the horizon of Boulder City. They did not notice an object in the sky until they edited the photographs. Then, to the photographer's surprise, a triangle-shaped object with a headlight appeared in the photos. The report claims that the craft had an ultraviolet color, helping it blend in with the black clouds.

The photographs revealed no light trails that airplanes normally create, and this led the photographer to believe the craft was stationary.

Other UFO reports include strange lights following the highway from Boulder City to Las Vegas.

There is a near-endless list of UFO reports on the MUFON website. In May 2020, more than ten were reported in the Vegas Valley area. Many of the stories are similar, but a few share no similar details to other reports in the area.[64]

Are these UFO sightings real? Could they be linked to Area 51? UFOlogists ask these questions when researching UFOs in the Nevada desert.

NOTES

Chapter 1

1. John Huck, "MGM Fire, Las Vegas's Worst Disaster Marks 40 Year Anniversary." FOX5 Las Vegas, https://www.fox5vegas.com.
2. Edmund Goulding, dir., *Grand Hotel* (Los Angeles, CA: Metro-Goldwyn-Mayer, 1932).

Chapter 2

3. Michael Solomon, "Luxury Lineage: A Brief History of Caesars Palace at 50," *Forbes*, August 3, 2016.
4. Bernie Wilson, "Ode to Evel: Pastrana Hopes to Clear Caesars Palace Fountain," *Las Vegas Sun*, July 6, 2018.

Chapter 3

5. Bryan Ke, "Vietnamese Couple Found Stabbed Inside Circus Circus Hotel in Las Vegas." NextShark, June 5, 2018. https://nextshark.com.
6. *LV Criminal Defense* (blog), "Violent Crime Continues in Las Vegas and Ghosts in Circus Circus." Las Vegas Criminal Lawyer: Wooldridge Law, June 8, 2018, https://www.lvcriminaldefense.com.

Chapter 4

7. Biography, "Tupac Shakur," December 4, 2017, https://www.biography.com.
8. Raul, "Tupac Shakur (2Pac) Shooting Location in Las Vegas, Nevada." FeelNumb, September 2, 2010, http://www.feelnumb.com.
9. History, "This Day in History. Tupac Shakur Is Shot," November 13, 2009, https://www.history.com.

Chapter 7

10. Haunted Places, "La Palazza Mansion," accessed October 14, 2022, https://www.hauntedplaces.org.

Chapter 8

11. Janice Oberding, *The Haunting of Las Vegas* (Gretna, LA: Pelican Publishing Group, 2008).

Chapter 9

12. Las Vegas Motor Speedway, https://www.lvms.com.
13. Aaron Ryan, "Las Vegas Crash Suspect Says the Ghost of Dale Earnhardt Told Him to Drive the Wrong Way," Whiskey Riff, February 2, 2022, accessed October 14, 2022, https://www.whiskeyriff.com.
14. Sabrina Schnur, "Coroner Identifies Man Found Outside Las Vegas Motor Speedway," *Las Vegas Review-Journal*, February 22, 2022.
15. Charles Bradley, "Wheldon Dies from Injuries," Autosport, October 16, 2011, accessed October 14, 2022, http://www.autosport.com.

Chapter 10

16. Natalie Keegan, "Lavish Life: How Did Liberace Die, What Was the Cause of Death and Who Is Scott Thorson?," *The Sun*, September 8, 2017.

17. The Liberace. Foundation for the Performing and Creative Arts, accessed October 14, 2022, https://liberace.org.

Chapter 13

18. Nevada State Parks, "Old Las Vegas Mormon Fort," http://parks.nv.gov.

Chapter 14

19. Steve Fishman, "The End of the Game," *New York*, accessed October 14, 2022, www.nymag.com.
20. Ed Koch and Jace Radke, "Questions Linger in Death of Actor," *Las Vegas Sun*, March 23, 1999.
21. "Famed Gambler Ungar Dies at 45," *Las Vegas Sun*, November 23, 1998.

Chapter 15

22. Las Vegas Online Entertainment Guide, "History of the Aladdin," accessed October 14, 2022, https://www.lvol.com.

Chapter 16

23. Historic Missourians, "Redd Foxx," accessed October 14, 2022, https://historicmissourians.shsmo.org.
24. "Marc Hoover: The Restless Spirit of Redd Foxx," *Clermont Sun*, November 8, 2018, https://www.clermontsun.com.

Chapter 17

25. Khalyleh, "We Hunted Ghosts in Famous Haunted Las Vegas Locations," *Reno Gazette Journal*.
26. CBS News, "Las Vegas Tunnels a Refuge for Homeless." January 4, 2010, accessed October 14, 2022, www.cbsnews.com.

27. Janice Oberding, *Haunted Las Vegas* (New Orleans, LA: Pelican Publishing, 2021).

Chapter 20

28. History, "This Day in History. Bugsy Siegel Opens Flamingo Hotel," www.history.com.
29. History, "This Day in History. Bugsy Siegel, Organized Crime Leader, Is Killed." www.history.com.
30. Robert Macy, "After 50 Years, Siegel Legend Haunts Resort," *Las Vegas Sun*, December 20, 1996, www.lasvegassun.com.

Chapter 21

31. Vegas Bright, "Luxor's Questionable Origins: The Crookedness of an Era Gone-by," March 29, 2016, www.vegasbright.com.
32. "Woman Commits Suicide Inside Luxor," *Las Vegas Sun*, September 26, 1996.
33. Cara McCoy, "Man Gets Life without Parole in Luxor Pipe Bomb Case," *Las Vegas Sun*, January 28, 2010.
34. Tiffany Gibson, "MMA Fighter Accused in Death of Ex-UNLV Football Player at Luxor," *Las Vegas Sun*, June 21, 2010.
35. "Airman Injured in Elevator Fall," CBS Las Vegas, March 27, 2012.
36. "Luxor Guests in Las Vegas Had Legionnaires'; Bacteria Found in Water after Guest Dies of Pneumonia," *New York Daily News*, January 31, 2012.
37. Titanic: The Artifact Exhibition, accessed October 14, 2022, https://www.titaniclasvegas.com.
38. Vegas News, "Titanic's Largest Recovered Artifact 'The Big Piece' at Titanic: The Artifact Exhibition," www.vegasnews.com, September 9, 2011.

Chapter 23

39. The Mob Museum, "The Mob Museum in Downtown Las Vegas," http://themobmuseum.org.

40. CBS Chicago, "Chicago Hauntings: Cursed Bricks, Noises, and Poltergeists Follow the Never-Prosecuted St. Valentine's Day Massacre," October 29, 2021, accessed October 14, 2022, https://www.cbsnews.com/chicago.

Chapter 24

41. Travel Channel, "Haunted Destination: The Riviera Hotel," accessed October 14, 2022, https://www.travelchannel.com.

Chapter 30

42. Zak Bagans' The Haunted Museum, "Historic, Reputedly-Haunted Landmark Featuring Zak Bagans' Personally Curated Cornucopia of the Macabre," https://thehauntedmuseum.com.
43. NPR, "Bela Lugosi's 'Dracula' Cape to Be Auctioned Off," November 1, 2011, accessed October 14, 2022, https://www.npr.org.
44. John Katsilometes, "Charles Manson's Ashes Used in Painting at Haunted Museum in Las Vegas," *Las Vegas Review-Journal*, July 30, 2018.
45. Keith Schneider, "Dr. Jack Kevorkian Dies at 83; Backed Assisted Suicide," *New York Times*, June 3, 2011.
46. Rhian Daly, "Post Malone Speaks about the Time He Was 'Cursed' by World's 'Most Haunted Object,'" NME, February 2, 2021.
47. John Philip Jenkins, "Ed Gein," Britannica, https://www.britannica.com.
48. Brie Schwartz, "Warning: Just Looking at This Haunted Doll Reportedly Triggers Sickness...Or Not," *Redbook*, April 17, 2015.
49. Sarah Bahr and Marisa Kwiatkowski, "Zak Bagans' 'Demon House' the Real Story: 10 Things to Know about the Gary, Indiana, Case," *Indianapolis Star*, February 16, 2019.
50. Crime Museum, "Ted Bundy," https://www.crimemuseum.org.

Chapter 31

51. Osie Turner, "What's beneath Sunset Park?," Living Las Vegas, February 5, 2016, https://living-las-vegas.com.

Chapter 32

52. "Zak Bagans, 'Ghost Adventures' Crew Investigate 'Very Haunted' Las Vegas Tiki Bar," *Las Vegas Review-Journal*, December 1, 2019.

Chapter 33

53. Scott Roeben, "Binion's Featured on Travel Channel's 'Ghost Adventures.'" Fremont Street Experience, February 26, 2019. https://vegasexperience.com.
54. Jackie Kostek, "Haunted Las Vegas: Paranormal Activity at Historic Hotel Apache," KTNV 13 Action News Las Vegas, October 28, 2020. https://www.ktnv.com.

Chapter 36

55. Eli Segall, "Building near Raiders Stadium Site Has Checkered, Possibly Haunted, History," *Las Vegas Review-Journal*, May 5, 2017.
56. Christian Cazares, "Iconic Las Vegas Hartland Mansion to Be Demolished," KLAS News Now, July 5, 2022, https://www.8newsnow.com.

Chapter 37

57. Travel Channel, "The World's 6 Best Hotspots to Hunt for Aliens and UFOs," May 25, 2021, accessed October 14, 2022, https://www.travelchannel.com.

Chapter 38

58. Clark County Nevada, "Clark County Museum," www.clarkcountynv.gov. https://www.clarkcountynv.gov.
59. "Ghosts Find Happy Haunting Grounds Here," *Las Vegas Review-Journal*, October 26, 2008.0

Chapter 39

60. The Mine Experience, accessed October 14, 2022, https://www.mccawmines.org.

Chapter 42

61. Ricardo Torres-Cortez, "Young Suspect Recounts Shooting Death of Teen at Abandoned Henderson Home," *Las Vegas Sun*, June 13, 2018.
62. Rio Lacanlale, "2 Sentenced to Life in Prison in Slaying of Henderson Teen," *Las Vegas Review-Journal*, December 10, 2019.

Chapter 48

63. UFO Stalker, "Black Triangle Sighting in Boulder City, Nevada on March 8th 1997—6 Lights Hovering over My Car Briefly, Silent and Probably a 'Big Black Delta,'" UFO World News, March 25, 2016, https://ufoworldnews.com.
64. MUFON—Mutual UFO Network, https://mufon.com.

BIBLIOGRAPHY

Adamakos, Tess. "Ghost Hunters Called to Investigate Haunted Las Vegas Tattoo Shop." Inked. October 30, 2018. Accessed October 12, 2022. https://www.inkedmag.com.

Anders, Allison, Alexandre Rockwell and Robert Rodriguez, dirs. *Four Rooms*. Los Angeles, CA: Miramax, 1995.

Biography.com. "Liberace." April 28, 2017. https://www.biography.com.

Boulder City Pet Cemetery. n.d. https://www.bouldercitypetcemetery.org.

Clark County Fire Department. "MGM Grand Hotel Fire Report." 1980. http://fire.co.clark.nv.us/(S(ucam3kt13pmcf2s1y3zimxrk))/Files/pdfs/MGM_FIRE.pdf.

Clarke, Norm. "Tragedy Follows 'Elvis' Show Work." *Las Vegas Review-Journal*, November 30, 2005.

Haunted Rooms. "Ballys Hotel & Casino, Las Vegas, Nevada." January 30, 2018. https://www.hauntedrooms.com.

Katsilometes, John. "Mixing Horror and Erotica at the Palomino Club Is a Delicate Dance." *Las Vegas Sun*, October 26, 2012.

Khalyleh, Hana. "We Hunted Ghosts in Famous Haunted Las Vegas Locations. Here's What We Found, and How." *Reno Gazette Journal*. Accessed October 17, 2019.

KTNV 13 Action News Las Vegas. "Haunted Las Vegas: Did Elvis Ever Really Leave the Westgate?" October 29, 2020. https://www.ktnv.com.

Las Vegas Review-Journal. "Man Dies after Jumping from the Strat." September 30, 2021.

———. "Man Jumps from Stratosphere Tower." February 8, 2006.

———. "News: In Brief." April 13, 2005.

———. "Zak Bagans' Haunted Museum Presents Creepy Collection in October." September 13, 2017.

Las Vegas Sun. "Boy, 16, Jumps from Stratosphere." July 15, 2002.

Leigh, Heather. *Haunted Southern Nevada Ghost Towns*. Charleston, SC: The History Press, 2022.

Morrison, Jane Ann. "Las Vegas News—Breaking News & Headlines." *Las Vegas Review-Journal*, November 20, 2005.

M2thaK. "The Haunted & Abandoned Three Kids Mine Field Wheel of Misfortune." YouTube. Accessed October 12, 2022. https://www.youtube.com/watch?v=ni7W5hnpx-w.

Oberding, Janice. *Haunted Nevada*. Mechanicsburg, PA: Stackpole Books, 2013.

Porter, Annalise. "Coroner Identifies Man Reported to Have Jumped from Stratosphere." *Las Vegas Review-Journal*, February 21, 2014.

Radke, Jace. 2000. "Man Jumps from Stratosphere Tower." *Las Vegas Sun*, January 7, 2000.

Slivka, Steven. "Police Investigate Possible Suicide near Stratosphere." 2014. *Las Vegas Review-Journal*, February 20, 2014.

Wolfpack Tattoo Las Vegas. Accessed January 21, 2017. http://wolfpacktattoo.com.

ABOUT THE AUTHOR

Heather Leigh Carroll-Landon, PhD, started her journey in the paranormal field as a teenager after multiple interactions with her grandfather, who passed away many years before. She has researched and traveled to locations to learn more about the history of the land, building and local area and paranormal claims. As long as she has been interested in the supernatural, Heather Leigh has been a freelance writer, writing for several newspapers, magazines and online publications.

Heather Leigh is the former chief administrative officer for the Warren Legacy Foundation for Paranormal Research and a ParaNexus Anomalous Research Association member. She and her family appeared in *Real Haunts: Ghost Towns* and *Real Haunts 3*, where they explored many southern Nevada ghost towns.

She is an author of articles and books and a lecturer about all things paranormal. Her first book, *Haunted Southern Nevada Ghost Towns*, was published by The History Press in August 2022.

She holds a doctor of philosophy degree in metaphysical and humanistic science with a specialty in paranormal science. She is a Certified Paranormal Investigator and a Certified EVP Technician. Her goal is to help others take a more scientific approach to paranormal investigations and research.

Heather Leigh is a cohost and content contributor for *Touch of Magick*, a podcast about magick and the supernatural, and she teaches classes through iMystic University. Heather Leigh is also the founder of Exploration Paranormal and host of *Exploring the Paranormal* on WLTK-DB Radio. She is also the cofounder of Witches Paranormal Society and cohosts *The Warren Files* and *Ghost Education 101* vodcasts on Facebook.

You can find Heather Leigh on Facebook (@DrHeatherLeigh), where you will find additional information, including upcoming classes, lectures and more. Or via her websites, www.heatherleighphd.com and www.explorationparanormal.com.